ALL HAPPY FAMILIES

ALL

HAPPY

FAMILIES

A Memoir

HERVÉ LE TELLIER

Translated from the French by Adriana Hunter

OTHER PRESS / NEW YORK

Originally published in French as *Toutes les familles heureuses*
in 2017 by Éditions Jean-Claude Lattès, Paris
Copyright © 2017 Éditions Jean-Claude Lattès
English translation copyright © 2019 Other Press

Production editor: Yvonne E. Cárdenas
Text designer: Jennifer Daddio / Bookmark Design & Media Inc.
This book was set in Centaur and Serlio
by Alpha Design & Composition of Pittsfield, NH

1 3 5 7 9 10 8 6 4 2

Library of Congress Cataloging-in-Publication Data

Names: Le Tellier, Hervé, 1957- author. | Hunter, Adriana, translator.
Title: All happy families : a memoir / Hervé Le Tellier ;
translated from the French by Adriana Hunter.
Other titles: Toutes les familles heureuses. English
Description: New York : Other Press, [2019] | "Originally published
in French as Toutes les familles heureuses in 2017
by Éditions Jean-Claude Lattès, Paris."
Identifiers: LCCN 2018031467 (print) | LCCN 2018056732 (ebook) |
ISBN 9781590519387 (ebook) | ISBN 9781590519370 (paperback)
Subjects: LCSH: Le Tellier, Hervé, 1957—Family. | Le Tellier, Hervé,
1957—Childhood and youth. | Authors, French—20th century—
Biography. | Authors, French—21st century—Biography. |
BISAC: BIOGRAPHY & AUTOBIOGRAPHY / Personal Memoirs. |
BIOGRAPHY & AUTOBIOGRAPHY / Literary. |
BIOGRAPHY & AUTOBIOGRAPHY / Women.
Classification: LCC PQ2672.E11455 (ebook) |
LCC PQ2672.E11455 Z46 2019 (print) | DDC 843/.914 [B]—dc23
LC record available at https://lccn.loc.gov/2018031467

FOR MELVILLE

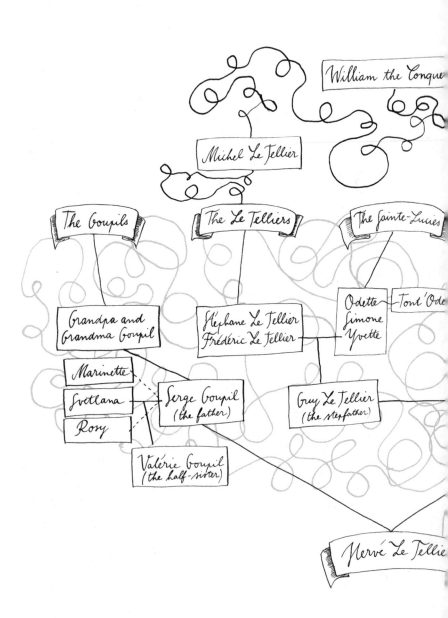

·FAMILY TREE·

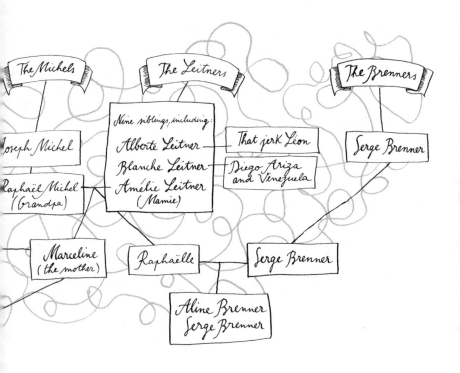

The Michels

The Leitners

The Brenners

Nine siblings, including:
Albertè Leitner
Blanche Leitner
Amélie Leitner
(Mamie)

That jerk Léon

Diego Ariza
and Venezuela

Joseph Michel

Raphaël Michel
(Grandpa)

Serge Brenner

Marceline
(the mother)

Raphaëlle

Serge Brenner

Aline Brenner
Serge Brenner

The wound is the place where the Light enters you

JALAL AD-DIN MUHAMMAD RUMI

ALL HAPPY FAMILIES

ONE

DIALECTIC OF
A MONSTER

Listen to your father, who gave you life,
and do not despise your mother when she is old.

PROVERBS 23:22

S o, apparently it's scandalous not to love your parents. Scandalous to wonder whether you should be ashamed because—despite your youthful efforts—you failed to find in your heart such a commonplace feeling as filial love.

A child's indifference is forbidden. Children are forever imprisoned by the love they spontaneously feel for their parents, whether the latter are good or cruel, intelligent or stupid, in a word, lovable or not. Behaviorists call these widely acknowledged, indisputable manifestations of affection "imprinting." An absence of filial love not only is an insult to decency, but also stabs in the back the edifice of cognitive sciences.

I was twelve years old. It must have been eleven o'clock in the evening and I was not yet asleep, because it was one of those very rare nights when my parents had gone out to dinner. Left alone, I was meant to be reading, probably Isaac Asimov, or Fredric Brown, or Clifford D. Simak. The telephone rang. My first thought was: it's the police, there's been a car crash, my parents are dead. I say "my parents" to simplify (you should always simplify), because I actually mean my mother and stepfather.

It wasn't the police. It was my mother. They were running late; she wanted to reassure me.

I hung up.

It occurred to me that I hadn't been worried. I'd imagined their demise with no feelings of panic or sadness. I was amazed to have so quickly accepted my status as an orphan, and appalled by the twinge of disappointment when I recognized my mother's voice.

That's when I knew I was a monster.

.
. .

I was informed that Serge had died one sunny afternoon. Serge was my father, my actual father. I was being driven to the Manosque literary festival. I remember that, as well as the driver, the car contained at least the poet Jean-Pierre Verheggen and the writer Jean-Claude Pirotte.

My cell phone rang; I didn't recognize the number and picked up. It was my sister. I say "my sister" when she is in fact my half sister, even though I've never been definitively conscious of having a half sister. She is seven or eight years younger than I am, the fact that my stepfather has adopted me means we don't have the same family name, and we must have met half a dozen times in our lives. Still, I did at some stage realize that she had burdened me with the heroic, mythologized mantle of the faraway big brother, an imaginary ceremonial garment that made me her brother while nothing succeeded in making her my sister. But I'd decided against pointing out this deceptive and elementary psychological truth to her. It was several years since we'd last spoken.

"Our father is dead," she said.

I watched the Provençal landscape spool past along the freeway, and found nothing to say in reply.

She and I both experienced a form of paternal absence, because I had never really known him, while she had left our father's house when she was fifteen to move in with her mother, and had rarely seen him since. In fact, this missing "father" compartment in both our lives was the only concrete subject of our very sporadic conversations. The difference between us was that I'd ended up resigned to his absence but she, who had spent her childhood with him, had never managed to come to terms with it and it pained her. On this particular morning, what she had actually lost was our absence of a father.

"Our father's dead," she said again.

"Really? When did he die?"

I was aware of silence settling over the car. That's often the effect you get with the word "die."

She told me briefly that he had been taken to the hospital for breathing difficulties, that his condition had deteriorated and he had died of an embolism in the night.

I made inquiries about practical details, the date and place of the funeral. I thought of offering her my condolences, but that seemed rather indelicate. I feigned sadness for another good minute, then hung up. Jean-Pierre Verheggen was watching me with some concern.

To reassure him, I said, "It's nothing. My father's dead."

Jean-Pierre laughed and that's when I knew I was a monster.

.

.   .

I was informed that my stepfather had died when I was called by Bichat Hospital while I was at the PEN Festival in New York. I'd set off for the United States when he'd already been in intensive care for a week. Still, his condition was not deemed to be life-threatening, and it didn't strike me as vital to stay in Paris to visit a man in an induced coma and pretend to support my mother. I called once a day and grasped that Guy's condition was deteriorating, with an endless round of alternating antibiotics and anti-inflammatories proving ineffectual and ultimately lethal. I was happier not being there. It would have been even more ignominious simulating affection than revealing my indifference to medical staff who have seen it all and can't be fooled.

I never liked my stepfather, and I can't believe that this absence of affection was not reciprocated. There was, as they say, no connection.

I was eighteen months old when he married my mother. The job of father was very much vacant, but he was in no hurry to snap it up, and anyway, I wasn't especially disposed to his taking it. In the end, the position was never filled. Some people will draw conclusions from reading the study by Pedersen et al. (1979) about a father's determining influence on a male child's cognitive development. For anyone else, let's say the father figure chose another route.

Guy and I never saw eye to eye. I have no recollections of tenderness, or empathy, and I can't have been much older than the age of reason when I decreed that he was a moron—a premature verdict, granted, but one that was not later invalidated.

I remember once unleashing a personal opinion at home. It must have been inadvertent because it wasn't something I did frequently, given that I was never satisfied by the debates prompted when I expressed my ideas. On this particular occasion, I was eleven; it was during the upheavals of May '68 and I'd made what—I admit—was a sweeping pronouncement, calling de Gaulle's minister for interior affairs, Michel Debré, a "dumbass." My stepfather retorted that "if he was such a dumbass he wouldn't be where he is." I immediately identified this statement as servile stupidity, although the formula that spontaneously came to mind was, "This guy's such a dumbass," which proves that the word "dumbass" came to me readily. I chose not to waste my time on an unproductive conflict, a decision that, on the threshold of adolescence (a phase well suited to so-called character-building confrontations), is proof in equal measures of wisdom and a superiority complex.

My stepfather respected every form of authority—be it hierarchical, police, or medical—and it so happens he also obeyed my mother. Weak with the strong, he was quite naturally strong with the weak. He was a teacher and enjoyed humiliating his pupils, taunting one in front of the others. That was his teaching method.

Born in late 1931, Guy was twelve when Paris was liberated at the end of World War II, twenty-five when events in Algeria stepped up a notch. A lucky generation but also a misbegotten one, their teenage years shoehorned between the Occupation and the Algerian War of Independence. He was born too late to collaborate with the Nazis, too soon to torture North Africans. There's nothing to prove he would have done either. Even performing despicable acts takes a bit of moral fiber. He probably wouldn't have had it in him to refuse climbing up into a watchtower.

My mother and Guy were that rare thing: a loveless codependent couple. She was never without him, he was never without her, they were never together.

Guy's death didn't bother her either way, except that it heralded true solitude on a day-to-day basis, and she could not yet envisage this for herself. On the other hand, it was crucial that she shouldn't be suspected of this indifference. Keeping up appearances was a social activity that had always strenuously mobilized her energy. Which is why my mother had gone to the hospital every day, because this—as she kept telling herself—was what duty required. She would take a sudoku and sit beside her deeply comatose husband, but boredom would settle in all too soon. She would resist it for a while, then couldn't help herself asking a nurse or a doctor for some excuse to justify her imminent departure. "I'll have to go home," she would say. "There's no point in my staying here, is there?" Bolstered by some such dispensation, she was then quick to flee.

So I heard that Guy had died when I was in New York. I handled administrative questions long-distance. Then I went home. For the funeral.

That's when I discovered that my mother was crazy.

Let's be clear on this.

I always knew my mother was crazy but I won't be discussing that here.

She had lost touch with reality long ago, but her husband managed everyday issues in such an orderly way that he had succeeded in disguising the evidence. After his death, my mother's madness descended into burlesque.

The morgue was almost deserted. There were five of us, maybe six.

The servants of death otherwise known as funeral parlor staff have a vocabulary all their own. My mother had hers too, a rather more immediate one. There was no common ground.

When the body had been laid out and nestled in the coffin's silk lining, one of the men in black came through to the waiting room and asked my mother gently, "Madame, would you like to view the deceased?"

"View him?" my mother asked indignantly. "He's not some house I'm thinking of buying, he's my husband!"

The man must have heard it all before, and he went on with his detailed protocol. He wanted to know whether we would like the coffin to stay slightly open so that, in keeping with a rather morbid tradition, family and friends could catch one last glimpse of the loved one. But this was how he put it:

"Would you like us to do an exhibition?"

"An exhibition of what?" my mother asked anxiously.

Then she added (and the rationality of it reassured her), "He had a lot of neckties."

The undertaker looked at her, perplexed.

Eventually the time came to screw down the lid. There was no one there anyway.

"We're closing, madame."

My mother glanced at her watch.

"Do you close for lunch?" she asked fretfully.

I laughed. And that's when I realized I was a monster.

TWO

THE STEPFATHER'S FUNERAL

There are people who are
granted a life by death.

LOUIS SCUTENAIRE, *MES INSCRIPTIONS*

I do hope I'll be forgiven for this meteorological chapter incipit, but it was the month of May and, as the temperature was over ninety degrees, the sidewalk outside the Paris church was almost deserted. We were waiting for the hearse.

You could argue that plenty of old people die alone, when their friends have died off before them one by one. But friends were something my parents didn't have. As a child, I was not surprised that no one, other than my grandparents and various cousins, ever visited us at home. For coffee, tea, or dinner. To a child, in the absence of any points of comparison, madness can appear to be the norm: after all, Romulus and Remus weren't in the least amazed to be raised by a she-wolf, Mowgli by a bear, or Tarzan by great apes. It was only later that I became aware of how strange my normality was.

It's fair to say that early on in their marriage, my mother and stepfather rented a very small Paris apartment, not very conducive to entertaining. But when I was nine they moved into a "character" apartment, as the ads like to call them, with a large tree-lined terrace looking out over the noisy boulevard Barbès and boulevard Ornano. It had unobstructed views of Montmartre and the Sacré-Coeur Basilica. This picture postcard setting could have made it a party venue, revolutionizing their social life. Nothing changed.

Occasionally—but this was very rare—my parents were invited for a meal by, let's call them acquaintances. I never saw my mother come home from one of these dinners anything but dissatisfied, disgruntled even. She would complain irritably, "To think we'll have to return the invitation."

My mother did not invite, she "returned" invitations. And it was a "pain in the ass."

So there was not one friend of the deceased on that sun-drenched sidewalk, and we waited for the hearse with just "close family," in other words relations of my son's mother along with my aunt, my cousins, and some of their children. Add to that the teenage faces of my son's friends who wanted to be there for him. Lastly, let's not forget the handful of people whose attendance could be deemed compulsory: an older man who occasionally did home improvements for them, and the gardener from their house in the country and his wife—who seemed genuinely sad.

Not one person there had been invited to my parents' fiftieth wedding anniversary celebrations a few years earlier. The Golden Wedding party had consisted of an excruciating trip in a *bateau-mouche* on the River Seine, for which too many canapés and too much champagne had been ordered, and where the guests—who had only very little to say to each other—were trapped together for the four hours of the cruise from Alma Bridge to Alma Bridge. It gave me a sort of parabolic summary of my teenage years, that needling sensation that yet again, if I wanted to jump ship, I'd have to throw myself in the water.

A woman in black, the back end of fiftysomething, came up to my mother to offer her condolences. I didn't know her, and my mother introduced her to me.

"This is Anna."

"Anja," the woman in black corrected her. "Anja Zewlakow."

"Yes, that's right," my mother went on. "Anna cleans my apartment for me. And she does it very well, in fact."

An indisputable way with a compliment. After this spontaneous tactlessness, my mother moved away and I stood alone with an embarrassed woman with downcast eyes. I said hello to her, putting as much courtesy and respect as I could muster into my eyes and gestures.

The turnover in my mother's cleaning ladies was substantial. They soon resigned, tired of being suspected of theft—my mother would leave wads of high-denomination bills lying around to test their honesty—or of the way she talked to them. Anja Zewlakow held on till the end of the year, thereby setting a world record of two years, which no one ever succeeded in wresting from her.

The hearse arrived at last and parked—or rather, double-parked—in front of the gate. Men in creased black suits alighted, opened the hatchback, and pulled out the coffin, lifting it by its brass handles to raise it onto their shoulders with a discreet "a-huh."

But this was a Paris church: cars were parked bumper to bumper, regardless of clear "No Parking" signs.

The head funeral director seemed in a quandary. In between a large German sedan and a Japanese hybrid, he had spotted a narrow space through which a slim man might just about pass. He tilted his chin toward it for the benefit of the other undertakers. They exchanged questioning glances, gauging the situation with consummate professionalism. I soon realized they thought the exploit possible: transporting what was at a conservative estimate a 260-pound coffin between the two cars, balancing it precariously as they walked in single file.

I immediately pictured the accident. The coffin would inevitably slip from their clutches, noisily caving in the hoods, destroying the windshields, perhaps even falling open? The amicable witness statement was bound to bring a smile to the faces of even the most progressive of car insurers: "I am coffin A. You are vehicle B."

I made the director aware of my considerable concern. He agreed not to take unnecessary risks and the men, still with the coffin on their shoulders, walked a good hundred feet to the end of the street, where there was a pedestrian crossing. When they reached the brasserie on the street corner they pivoted around ninety degrees. People sipping coffee under parasols on the terrace looked disconcerted, worried. Some of them, ruffled to see death pass only feet from where they were seated, put down their coffee cups.

Nevertheless, the entire scene unfolded with the utmost dignity.

Camus summarized his book *The Stranger* in one sentence: "In our society, any man who doesn't cry at his mother's funeral is liable to be condemned to death." If the Nobel laureate speaks the truth, my aunt Raphaëlle was in no danger whatsoever. She wept. My mother's sister has always cried at funerals. It's in her nature. You could have buried a hamster she'd once met and she wouldn't have cried any less.

Her conspicuous sobbing irritated my mother. She gave a shrug as she glowered at her sister, who was somehow robbing her of her grief.

"Don't you think she's exaggerating just a bit?" she hissed, suddenly furious. "Anyone would think it was *her* husband who died."

An hour later, as my aunt leaned over the book of condolences, she must have been sincere but also a little thoughtless when she wrote: "to my brother-in-law whom I love. Raphaëlle."

She didn't realize at the time how my mother would interpret these words. But we mustn't get ahead of ourselves.

THREE

RACHMANINOV'S CONCERTO NO. 2

I may be laughing, but I'm not
doing it on purpose.

ERIK SATIE, *LA JOURNÉE DU MUSICIAN*

Marfan syndrome is a disorder of the connective tissue. It affects about one person in every five thousand. The gene whose mutation produces the condition is on chromosome 15, and the mutation can have nearly a thousand variants. Symptoms of the syndrome include aortal aneurism, pronounced nearsightedness, and unusual bone growth. Sufferers are often very tall with long, thin fingers.

The British actor Peter Mayhew, famous for playing the hairy Wookiee Chewbacca in the *Star Wars* movies, has the syndrome. Some claim that Abraham Lincoln did too. But that is of no concern to us here.

The composer and pianist Sergey Rachmaninoff suffered from it, if the December 1986 edition of the *British Medical Journal* is to be believed. The condition goes some way to explaining his virtuosity, his ability to play chords spread very wide across the keyboard. The maximum spread of a pianist's fingers, from thumb to little finger, is often around eight and a half inches, which allows for playing ninths with ease. Rachmaninov's hand-span was around twelve inches. His Piano Concerto no. 3 in D Minor, op. 30, includes elevenths that must be played with one hand, and its reputation as the world's most difficult work to perform has earned it the nickname "Rach 3" in the same way as we say "Mach 3" for three times the speed of sound.

But it is his Piano Concerto no. 2 in C Minor, op. 18, composed in 1901, that enjoys the greatest success. An eight-bar opening for solo piano, a slow series of chords in crescendo until the orchestra starts to play. Its melody has become popular and has featured in dozens of films, including one by Lelouch, and thousands of ice dancers have fallen flat on their faces to the *adagio sostenuto* second movement.

The second concerto is not significantly less arduous to play than the Rach 3. Here too there are tenths to span. Hands too small for the task exhaust themselves attempting it. It is, however, possible to improve, the body is compliant: after years of working their repertoire, which requires the left hand to stretch more, most pianists notice this hand gaining half an inch of span. It is also possible to cheat, which is what all the virtuoso Chinese women pianists do, playing a brisk arpeggio rather than spanning the whole chord.

Standing in pride of place in the middle of our living room was an ebony black baby grand piano, a Schimmel. It was less an instrument, more a cumbersome ornament, a dark, lacquered thing, which, mathematically speaking, took up at least one twentieth of the apartment's total floor space, a sufficiently large percentage to demonstrate our musical erudition to our very rare visitors. But my stepfather played very little. Except, occasionally, this diabolical second concerto of Rachmaninoff's. To be completely frank, Guy played nothing *but* Rachmaninoff's second concerto, alas practicing too infrequently to master other pieces. He was not a very tall man with hands in proportion, and he will have arpeggiated the chords, for sure. In fact, he must once have played it rather well, because he could still perform a few fleeting dazzling bars. He played it less and less, until the day when his pleasure was drowned out by the wrong notes and he resigned himself to never playing it again.

He continued to listen to it, though. In the recording by Sviatoslav Richter, with long and hypnotic dramatic crescendos. Or the one by Rafael Orozco, a lush, generous performance, too much so, even, some would say. Perhaps also Vladimir Ashkenazy's, which is wonderfully intense but where the soloist sometimes seems to forget there is an orchestra at all. But that's of little consequence: Have I mentioned that my stepfather loved this concerto? To the point that he'd told my mother that, when the time came for him to leave this world, as he lay on his deathbed, he would like to listen to it one last time.

What would I myself like to listen to in the final moments of my life? Now that I think about it, perhaps not music. A friend's voice, or my son's, or the voice of a woman I love. I don't know. My ears will probably strain to catch an unexpected sound instead, an incongruous sound produced at random, a sound that still belongs to the living world, a nurse laughing at the duty desk, an impatient car horn from the street, or just the click-clack of heels on a tiled floor. Perhaps there are still vestiges of sound before the last cells fade out for good. I'll take whatever's going.

Neither do I know which last musical memory I would like to leave for my loved ones, in what they call my farewell ceremony. Leonard Cohen's "Hallelujah" definitely feels too unoriginal, even performed by Rufus Wainwright. What I'd like—at a time that is yet to be determined—is Bob Dylan's original version of "Knockin' on Heaven's Door," or his duet of it with Bruce Springsteen. "Peter Gunn Theme" from *The Blues Brothers*, a pretty flamboyant piece, would be quite a good accompaniment for a cremation. These are just suggestions. Mind you, in an ideal world, the composer of the music for my funeral has not yet even been conceived.

In any event, my stepfather had at some point mentioned this second concerto as the music to launch him into the hereafter. He is taken to the hospital on April 2 for what is diagnosed as an intestinal hemorrhage. On the morning of the 4th he is intubated and tired but conscious. The medical staff are trying to find a cause and an effective treatment, although they are not yet concerned about the outcome and won't give any prognosis. There is nothing more straightforward than hospital logic: sufficient unto the day is the evil thereof.

In the afternoon I join my mother at Bichat. She is sitting next to her husband's bed, her sudoku book on her lap. My stepfather has his eyes closed and headphones over his ears.

She immediately tells me, in a voice that blends the appropriate note of tragedy with the pride of a duty accomplished, "I've put on Rachmaninov's Concerto Number Two for him."

If he was conscious at the time, Guy must have thought it was a little premature, a sign of impatience even.

But it was not long before my mother was proved right.

FOUR

GRANDPA

The present would be full of every future
if the past had not already projected
History onto it.

ANDRÉ GIDE, *LES NOURRITURES TERRESTRES*

The planet that was our family orbited around a sun: my grandfather Raphaël, my mother's father. His surname was Michel. Which made him Raphaël Michel. Raphaël meaning "God has healed." Michel meaning "Who is like God?" Heavy symbolism, but we spoke little Hebrew at home, and to me he was Grandpa. Undisputed patriarch and the only solid foundation through my childhood: "Grandpa, that hero with the sweetest smile" was my personal refrain.

Raphaël was born at the turn of the twentieth century in German Moselle country. His mother took in sewing work; his father, Joseph, was a craftsman. I met this great-grandfather because he lived to nearly a hundred, despite his considerable consumption of Niñas, revolting thin cigars whose smell impregnated all his clothes.

He was a small, wiry man, taciturn and stubborn. My instincts told me to be afraid of him, and I thought twice about approaching him for fear of being walloped, a word as old as he was. I was fascinated that he'd been born two years after the Paris Commune. In 1914 he was already too old to enlist, but if he could have, he would have done so on the Kaiser's side, because that was the side on which his heart beat, as did—despite accepted French mythology—the hearts of many from Alsace-Lorraine.

At his funeral, when I was thirteen, I learned from my grandmother that so long as he had had the strength in him, Joseph had beaten his wife and mistreated his two sons, Raphaël and Émile. She also told me that in 1940, when Joseph knew he would be leaving his house in Picardy to join his son in Paris, he put down his dog without a moment's hesitation and threw the body on the manure heap, which did not yet go by the name of "compost." It was this last image that struck me most.

Raphaël found no better way to escape his brutal father than to enlist in the navy at eighteen, just after the war. It was on a naval cruiser that he learned his trade as a mechanic and studied as an engineer. It was also at sea that he lost his hair: at the age of twenty, the strapping fellow was bald, but his regular features and square chin coped well with baldness. He left the navy in the mid-1920s to return to Lorraine, which was now entirely French, and he moved to Jœuf, a market town where he found work repairing rolling stock for the mines. The collapse of the metalworking industry may be draining Jœuf of its inhabitants now, but in the thirties the town thrived on its foundry. The owners, the De Wendel family, still have a château and even a church, which was built at the turn of the last century for their workforce, some of them French but mostly Poles and Italians.

It was in Jœuf that Raphaël met Amélie, the daughter of modest Alsace farm stock, the Leitners, the fifth of nine children. He courted her, won her heart, and married her. Raphaëlle was born a few months later.

The Leitner family was poor, but it had a South American fairy tale: Blanche, the eldest child, had worked as a nurse on the French side during the First World War and had tended one Diego Ariza, a Panamanian officer, and fallen in love with him. I'll come back, he'd promised her. From the letters he wrote her, he appeared to have returned to Panama, then moved to New York, and finally immigrated to Maracaibo in Venezuela, where he soon made a fortune in oil. People in Jœuf gently poked fun at Blanche with her Panamanian, right up until—true to his word—he came back in 1920 to ask for her hand. The couple treated themselves to a spectacular wedding with hundreds of guests: the small town partied for a whole week. Blanche went off to Maracaibo to live like a queen and have three children. Their considerable standing was not a family invention: in the sixties, to the amazement of their French cousins, you could address an envelope to "Blanche Ariza-Leitner, Maracaibo, Venezuela," and have no concerns about the letter getting lost.

In search of some roots, the Arizas liked nothing better than crossing the Atlantic to visit their distant Leitner cousins and also my grandmother Amélie, who was Blanche's favorite sister. One morning their plane had just landed on the tarmac at the brand-new Roissy airport, and they called my mother. She had unwillingly invited all five of them to join us for a day in the country. She really hoped she had dissuaded them but when we reached the house they were already there waiting for us, laden with presents. They had simply taken two taxis, and the drivers—whose meters kept on turning energetically—declined the invitation to have lunch, choosing instead to wait at the truck stop until the family finally decided, around nightfall, to head back to Paris.

"I wonder how much that's costing them, it's madness," my mother kept saying to my grandmother, who was presiding over the kitchen.

But money was the least of their concerns: as soon as Concorde began its weekly Paris–Caracas flights, the Venezuelan cousins came even more regularly. My mother told me that, as a twentieth birthday present, they'd very much like me to visit them and they would even pay for my supersonic return flight. I declined.

"You're crazy to turn this down," she said. "You'll never be able to afford it yourself."

My mother took pleasure in broadcasting the fact that the Leitners were illiterate, given that stating it made her own ascent all the more glorious. The truth is that, having been born in Alsace in the days of the Reich, they were more familiar with German than French. My very fat Great-Aunt Alberte, who was always wedged in her armchair and didn't smell too good, had retired from her job for "Shtomm," a company whose name she pronounced with such a strong accent that it was a long time before I realized she meant Alsthom.

True, my grandmother struggled to read, sometimes following the lines with her finger. But she bought *France-Soir*—"a million copies a day"—every morning, and did her crosswords; and on Mondays she bought *Détective*, a gossipy weekly with improbable headlines...oh, those "he drugged his wife and auctioned her naked"s! I discovered later that this periodical was founded before the war by Gaston Gallimard and the Kessel brothers, and that André Gide, Georges Simenon, and Albert Londres freelanced for it back in the day.

Amélie Leitner, "Mamie" to my cousins and me, was a gentle, self-effacing woman utterly devoted to her husband, her daughters, and her grandchildren. Mamie dealt with the housework, the dishes, the ironing, the shopping, and the cooking, and she often took me to school and picked me up again: so she never did a day's work in her life. To kick-start a day like that she would have her little cup of black coffee at the local bistro, Le Repaire. She also smoked Winstons and drank Valstar, a now discontinued beer that was the cheap and cheerful choice of the likes of the working-class Groseille family in the film *La vie est un long fleuve tranquille*. She sometimes poured me a glass of it, tempering the alcohol with Dumesnil lemonade.

She was probably already living this same rather tedious, hardworking life in the thirties when she raised her daughters, Raphaëlle and Marceline. The sisters were born before the crash of 1929, and when the full force of the crash hit Europe, Raphaël found an unusual job that took him away from his wife and daughters for a whole year: he became one of the eight mechanics on Citroën's "Yellow Tour," a major scientific and promotional expedition across Asia in 1931. A few years earlier, the car manufacturer had organized a "Black Tour," in Africa; political correctness was yet to be invented. In April 1931 Raphaël set off from Beirut for the Persian Gulf, on board one of Citroën's seven tracked vehicles. They were to meet up in Peking, which was not yet Beijing, where they would be joined by the philosopher Pierre Teilhard de Chardin. My grandfather treasured his beautiful scrapbook of that year in the Gobi Desert, Xinjiang, and the Himalayas, and reproductions of gouache illustrations by the expedition's official painter, Alexandre Jacovleff, hung in his living room. By the time my grandfather returned he had a reputation for fine-tuning engines, and was soon snapped up by Simca car manufacturers, who had a plant in Nanterre. Simcas were then nothing other than clones of small Fiat models, including the first Fiat 500, renamed the Simca 5.

That is how the Michels left Lorraine and moved to Paris, to a tiny one-bedroom apartment on the boulevard Ornano, in the Eighteenth Arrondissement. When I read Modiano's novel *Dora Bruder* some twenty years ago now, I strongly suspected my grandparents lived in the same building as the heroine. For a while I was afraid I'd spent my early years in an apartment stolen from a Jewish family. Even the telephone number seemed familiar: ORN-49-20.

But it wasn't the same address. Dora Bruder lived at number 41, we at number 16. And her phone number was ORN-48-05. Still, what does that prove? Nothing. There were so many Dora Bruders. This retrospective fear speaks volumes about my respect for our family values and our ethics in general. Let's say it was a moderate sort of respect.

In 1940, Raphaël found two garret rooms in the building and persuaded his parents to come to the capital: they'd never been happy in the house he'd bought for them in Picardy, equidistant between him in Paris and his brother, Émile, in Péronne. A few years later he set up an apartment on the sixth floor for his wife's sister—my huge

Great-Aunt Alberte—and her husband, Léon, whom he privately referred to as "thajerléon," a term I initially interpreted with some bafflement as "thatcher Léon," before grasping that it was of course "that jerk Léon."

The Second World War came to an end. Rather unfairly, the only company accused of collaborating was Renault, when the whole car industry had in fact worked for the Germans, including the American company Ford. The Franco-Italian Simca also made a substantial contribution to the Nazi war effort, but I know nothing of my grandfather's participation because my mother's answers were always evasive.

In the late 1940s Raphaël was taken on by Panhard as an engineer. The former mechanic had become an engineer thanks to the Arts et Métiers technical college in Paris, the only grande école offering in-house training. His default setting was to despise the alumni of the far more exciting Polytechnique, people who could lay claim to the prestigious nickname X and who, "if they need boiling water, will boil water, but if they need warm water, they'll also boil water so they're back with a known problem. Then they leave it to cool."

As a swaggering, seductive, good-looking man, he was publicly acknowledged to have cheated on Amélie the whole time. One affair must have gone beyond all the others, because he made up his mind to admit to Amélie that he'd met another woman and the relationship was "important."

I know nothing about this woman except that, according to my mother, she was "younger by ten years." Every time my mother mentioned her, she never worded it in any other way than "younger by ten years." Not "he was ten years older than she was" or "she was ten years younger than him," or perhaps "they had a ten-year age difference." No, the words were fixed as "youngerbytenyears," and the hypnotic repetition of them screened off the reality of a woman who surely wouldn't recognize herself in this summary.

Raphaël wanted a divorce. His wife, who could not imagine a life without him, was devastated. But that was nothing: their twenty-year-old daughter Marceline stopped talking and eating. She went on strike from life and underwent an emergency hospitalization. When she was sent home from the clinic two weeks later there was no more talk of separation, and Raphaël stayed with Amélie. For some time, though, he led a double life, splitting himself between two households. It was unlivable, and the other woman—who as we know was youngerbytenyears—eventually left him. At least that's the official version. Various clues and allusions hint that they stayed in touch to the end.

Life picked up again on the boulevard Ornano. Raphaëlle started "stepping out" with young men and even became engaged; my mother continued her studies. Her demented reaction to the prospect of her parents' separation had inevitably worried Raphaël, but he was unwilling to have her fragile mental state assessed because he mistrusted anything remotely like a psychiatrist. He was relieved when a few months later she met the man who was to become my father, and was thoroughly relieved when she married him, a few months after her older sister Raphaëlle's wedding. It must have been a source of great pride to him that both his sons-in-law were real "*Gadz'arts*": they had diplomas from Arts et Métiers, having gained entrance to the college via the illustrious route of passing the entrance exam.

The beginning of the "Glorious Thirty," the three decades of economic growth after the war, coincided with my grandfather's social advancement. It was at about this time that, according to my mother, he became Jean Panhard's "right-hand man," lunching with him "every day" and apparently frequently inviting him home for dinner. But how to believe this? The name Raphaël Michel does not feature in any organization charts of the management team from that period. My mother also told me he designed the PL17 and the Panhard CD, then, having moved to Citroën when Panhard was bought out in 1965, he contributed to the Citroën DS adventure—a feat that was chronologically impossible. Here again, a daughter's pride has generously colored reality. In any event, he evidently climbed a long way up first Panhard's and then Citroën's hierarchy, because his company car was always the handsomest big-cylinder model available, including a magnificent metallic sand-colored DS 21: I have him to thank for a fairly pronounced passion for cars and I still have a comfortable chair in buffalo leather that is actually the front seat of a DS mounted on welded steel pipes. He most likely ran one of the "engine" divisions, and it's also likely that the constant levels of benzene in his work environment were responsible for the leukemia that killed him.

Raphaël wanted his daughters and sons-in-law closer to him: he instituted rituals for each of their birthdays, the summer vacation, and the Christmas holidays. My mother couldn't have wished for anything better. In fact, she never succeeded in breaking away from her parents, living never more than a stone's throw away, while the big wide world beckoned Raphaëlle, who was quick to move away.

When my mother separated from my father, she descended into depression again. My grandfather took her in for a while, to spare her another hospitalization. Then he arranged for her to travel to England: in just a few weeks he found her a job as a French teacher at a junior high school in a South London suburb, along with on-site accommodation, and he insisted that I should stay in Paris with him and my grandmother, while she recovered from the "shock." It was an extreme suggestion, but he felt it was right to protect me. He thought this English interlude would last a few months—but I stayed with my grandparents longer than he'd imagined.

When my mother came back she had become Madame Le Tellier. Raphaël, meanwhile, had become "Grandpa": my cousin had just been born so he now had three grandchildren, a status that delighted him. I'm not sure how this happened, but he even became "Grandpa" to his new son-in-law Guy, who thereby entered into a peculiar denominative parity with me—which also constituted an acknowledged act of submission on his part.

Not long after this, Raphaël wanted to move house: he bought off-plan a two-bedroom apartment in a building under construction on the corner of boulevard Barbès and rue Ordener, and immediately suggested Guy and my mother should buy an apartment in the same building. She quickly agreed. Property prices in Paris then still allowed a couple of teachers to pay off a mortgage in fifteen years. That is how my parents came to move to the eighth and highest floor and my grandparents to the sixth; short of actually living together, the seventh would have been more logical, but a third party had been swifter on the uptake. My mother offered an exchange with my grandparents' apartment but the man tartly refused what would have been a foolish trade-off: on the sixth floor the seventh-floor balcony would block out the sky and, being ten feet lower down, he would have lost his view of Sacré-Coeur. This neighbor, who unduly separated my mother from her parents, became her bête noire, and she made him suffer for it at every co-ownership meeting.

The kitchen in our eighth-floor apartment was tiny, but we didn't use it because we didn't have a dining room, only two bedrooms and a large living room with the piano but no table. We ate lunch and supper with Grandpa and Mamie. I was the one best pleased with this situation; I spent all my time in my grandfather's apartment, which is where my toys, building kits, and puzzles were. It was also here that I read large bound and illustrated "Nature" albums of *Life* magazine. My favorite was *Living Desert*, full to bursting with pit vipers, cacti, and jerboas. When it was time for bed, I climbed the two flights of stairs in my pajamas and went straight to sleep. It was almost always my grandmother who came to wake me. Nothing about this unusual setup struck me as unusual.

I owe it to the truth to say that Grandpa wasn't always entirely honorable. I've chosen to forget his contempt for "North Africans," farming stock who became "the muscles of France": three thousand of them working for Panhard at porte de Choisy, and thirty-five hundred for Citroën at quai de Javel. It was in our very house that I first heard the word "*crouille*," which was originally a civility derived from the word "*khuya*," for "my brother," but had become an insult. Shortly after Raphaël died, I talked about this with my mother: "He was of his time," she said forgivingly. I disagreed.

Then came his leukemia. It took hold of him when he reached retirement age, and gave him only three years to live. He didn't talk about it much, or at least never in front of me. He squared up to it as best he could, preparing to die. On his nightstand there were fewer and fewer books by Balzac and Hugo, and more and more by Seneca, Cicero, and Epicurus, along with the Bible. But when asked if he'd like a religious funeral, he would shrug. Religion was his final curiosity. I still have his copy of the Koran, annotated in pencil.

My last memory of my grandfather is not in the hospital. He didn't want his grandchildren witnessing his slow death throes. It was one morning in the country, when I came across him getting dressed in his bedroom: I saw a stooped old man, his body covered with pressure sores, embattled by a cancer whose progress wasn't slowed at all by his transfusions. I looked away, utterly crushed by the double realization that he was mortal and was close to death. I ran into the garden, down to the hazelnut bushes in the hedge at the bottom, to cry, and cry, unable to stop.

FIVE

MARCELINE

This, then, was our youth,
the deep morning
never to be regained.

PATRICK MODIANO, *LA PLACE DE L'ÉTOILE*

My mother was born exactly a week after Audrey Hepburn, and about 150 miles away as the crow flies, because the English-speaking actress was born in Ixelles in Belgium, and my mother in Jœuf in Lorraine. What might have been…

I know almost nothing about her younger years, and it's complicated for me looking into who the woman that was my mother actually was. I know she was a shy, diffident, nervous child. You have to imagine a little girl who lived in the shadow of a bold, tempestuous older sister of whom she was terribly jealous, although she dared not identify her feelings as such yet. Until late into her teens she had disturbed nights. She suffered appalling nightmares, night terrors that woke her, and bouts of sleepwalking. At fourteen she was found out on the balcony in the middle of the night, muttering incomprehensibly. From that day forward, windows were locked overnight.

When the Michels moved to Paris, Marceline and her sister were enrolled at Jules-Ferry High School. The sisters arrived fresh from Lorraine with a coarse accent that they soon lost. Perhaps they took the Métro at Marcadet-Poissonniers and changed at Pigalle. But it's far more likely they walked and Raphaëlle was given charge of her younger sister. Place Clichy, where their school was, is the gateway to the Paris of Céline, a neighborhood full of craftsmen and workmen and others shipped in from the suburbs by tram, an endless round of employment and redundancy.

In 1941 the German occupation put its imprint on the landscape. My mother was twelve, my aunt fourteen. The large Café Wepler opposite their school was requisitioned and set up as a *Soldatenheim*, accommodation for German soldiers. *"Speise und Aufenthalstraüme"* (meals and lounge areas), announced a huge sign some sixty-five feet long: you couldn't miss it. Dozens of soldiers came and went at any given moment; they smoked on the sidewalk and struck up conversations with young women: Paris was theirs. My aunt remembers this. My mother does not.

The roundups of Jews began in the summer and autumn of 1942. I was in junior high when I learned about the extermination, which wasn't called that in the sixties; it wasn't yet called the Shoah. People talked about deportations, and concentration camps. And yet these were *Vernichtungslager,* annihilation camps. No one at home had ever told me about it. In 1969, I myself was twelve and in ninth grade. The long reign of the Malet-Isaac history manuals was coming slowly to an end, but the Second World War was on the syllabus only for senior year. The school's film club showed Alain Resnais's documentary *Night and Fog.* Behind me, some teenagers made the most of the dark to kiss.

I learned the whole story. I was shocked, horrified. The image of bulldozer buckets transporting bodies was engraved on me forever. If I had to give a start date for my political commitment, it would be that day. I didn't realize it at the time but when *Night and Fog* was made in 1956, censors had insisted that the instantly recognizable peaked cap of a French gendarme be obscured on a guard at Pithiviers camp. Since February the attorney general had been one François Mitterrand. It was vitally important that the French State's responsibility be obscured, along with the ignominy of Laval's government when he signed off on the deportation of children under sixteen even though the Nazis themselves did not insist on this. I also discovered later that it was the actor Michel Bouquet who had read Jean Cayrol's voice-over text; as an homage to the victims, he asked for his name not to appear in the credits.

Despite the courage of two young literature teachers, Annette Maignan and Andrée Pauly-Santoni, who hid a few children in their own homes, Jules-Ferry High School saw twenty-four Jewish pupils deported to Pithiviers or Drancy, and then on to Auschwitz. Not one came back. Their names were Mira Adler, Nicole Alexandre, Jacqueline Berschtein, Alexandra Cheykhode, Fortunée Choel, Paulette Cohen, Renée Cohen, Paulette Goldblatt, Thérèse Gradsztajn, Rosette Hayem, Marceline Kleiner, Janine Lubetzki, Estelle Moufflarge, Colette Navarro, Huguette Navarro, Ethel Orloff, Giberte Rabinowitz, Rose Rosenkrantz, Françoise Roth, Jacqueline Rotszyld, Jacqueline Rozenbaum, Marguerite Margo Scapa, Rose-Claire Waissman, and Olga Zimmerman.

During the 1941–42 academic year, Paulette Goldblatt was in the same class as Raphaëlle, seventh grade BI. Her father was a tailor and dress designer, and she lived with him at 72 Boulevard Ornano. She was deported to Auschwitz on September 14, 1942, in convoy number 32. Paulette lived three hundred yards from the Michel sisters, on the same side of the street. They can't have not traveled to and from school together. But neither Raphaëlle nor Marceline remembers her.

That same year Rose Rosenkrantz was in my mother's class, sixth grade A3. She was just a month younger than little Marceline. She lived alone with her mother, Liba, a seamstress, at 14b rue Lemoine in the Seventeenth Arrondissement; her father had died in the thirties. During the roundup at the Vél d'Hiv cycling stadium on

July 16 and 17, 1942, she was arrested with her mother. They were interned at Beaune-la-Rolande camp, transferred to Drancy, and finally deported to Auschwitz in convoy number 76. My mother was thirteen. She doesn't remember little Rose either, Rose who never made it into seventh grade.

I have no explanation for this amnesia. After seeing *Night and Fog*, I came home still shivering from the atrocious images, with Michel Bouquet's metallic voice resonating. I asked questions, dozens of them. We didn't know, my mother said. I was too young, my stepfather added. My grandmother was evasive. My grandfather was dead, and who knows what he would have said.

Perhaps the crime was so total, so inconceivable, and those two children so powerless that their urge to forget worked its slow way to erasing memories. Perhaps also their parents were afraid of terrorizing their young daughters. Alas, I suspect that in the Michel household, the monstrosity taking place under their very noses was never a topic of conversation. Following on from that, I heard my mother trot out trivial clichés about "the Jews" who were "rich" and "looked after each other" too many times not to conclude that she was at best indifferent. In our household the war appears to have been condensed into a few deprivations and plenty of frustrations.

My mother had just celebrated her fifteenth birthday when Paris was liberated by Leclerc's tanks. The capital was in party mode but she would never have followed her sister on her nocturnal escapades: she was as wary of the tall, keen allied GIs as she had been of the German occupiers. In the evenings she went home to her parents like a good girl, back to the little family apartment, and crossed paths with her sister, who was heading out. Marceline worked hard and went to bed early but still procrastinated the moment she would fall asleep and confront her nightmares. And anyway she was woken by her sister when she returned home.

Marceline's schoolwork was mediocre. She was neither stupid nor a bad pupil, but the stress of exams robbed her of all ability. She only just passed her baccalaureate and went on to the Sorbonne to study English. But the supervisory structure of high school suited her better than the freedom of university: she got lost in corridors, couldn't find her room, missed classes, and floundered as soon as there was a deadline to deliver work. Being hardworking, she eventually gained her degree and started teaching English while she finished her studies.

She was reserved, and frightened of everyone. And if her own father hadn't insisted she accompany her sister to a *Gadz'arts* ball, she would never have met Serge, my future begetter. He was no less shy than she was. It established a connection.

It was not long before Marceline married him and moved out of the paternal home for the conjugal one, very close by. So close that the newlyweds ate at my mother's parents' house every evening, or nearly. Serge and Marceline also joined my grandparents in the country every weekend. My grandfather liked this son-in-law who was deft with his hands, an engineer, so like him. When Alzheimer's made my mother forget everything right down to her very long-standing fury with Serge, she never stopped saying that those years spent in a cocoon between her father and her husband had been "the best of her life."

It lasted six years. My mother found she was pregnant. I was born.

•
• •

L ook, it's your daddy." A new baby is always introduced to his or her father. The mother, never. Why would you? The baby has been inside her, is a natural extension of her. The serious misunderstanding that ensued has its origins in this strange preconception.

So I was born, then.

The happy event was badly timed. I don't know how long love lasts, but my father had met another woman. My mother discovered the betrayal and drove him out, then her world fell apart: in her fury she broke the entire contents of the house down to the tiniest thing. And then she collapsed.

She took refuge with her parents, lying prostrate, refusing all contact with my father. She was having a nervous breakdown and could no longer cope with giving lessons. She sometimes left me alone, failed to look after me. Or, conversely, she would take me in her arms, cradling me and humming to me for so long that my grandmother had to wrest me from her. She fluctuated between fits of destructive rage and uninterrupted sobbing, and then would abruptly descend into silence. Her anxious father made all her decisions for her. He persuaded her to leave France, and she obeyed him. It was meant to be temporary. Temporary kept going, and my first word was of course "Mamie."

SIX

MY SISTER
THE WHORE

We must obey our parents, sister;
a father has full power over us.
MOLIÈRE, *LES FEMMES SAVANTES*

M y sister's a whore," my mother took to saying when the flood barrier of decorum gave way to age and dementia, and she stopped feigning affection.

This whore was also my godmother. My mother admitted she'd never loved her, perhaps precisely because Raphaëlle was so lovable.

It was to this first daughter that my grandfather had so generously bequeathed his name. A happy, boisterous girl, she remained his favorite. Raphaëlle was only eighteen months older than Marceline but numbers are deceptive. There was nearly a decade between them: my aunt was a woman at thirteen, my mother not until she was twenty. The younger sister's body rejected puberty for a long time: she had watched Raphaëlle grow and launch herself into an adult world that frightened her, Marceline, and had refused to join her there. Being less lively, less cheerful, less pretty, she could never have competed with her.

So when Paris was liberated in August 1944, Raphaëlle was a zesty, intrepid woman of seventeen, and Marceline a rather withdrawn prepubescent girl of fifteen. In a capital fizzing with celebrations, Raphaëlle discovered life and love. She'd found herself a brazen accomplice in her cousin Lucie, who was just older than she was, and together they explored the city's streets, accepting offers of cigarettes from Allied soldiers. As my mother would say on the rare occasions when she mentioned those days, the pair of them "painted the town red."

Raphaëlle was not yet twenty when she met an American officer. She immediately became utterly besotted and, no less quickly, utterly pregnant. Alas, flustered by the news of this pregnancy, the man admitted that he was married and actually had two children already. To convince the tearful young woman, he had to produce photographs of his wedding in Brooklyn and his two sons. "What do you expect…" my mother would say later with spiteful glee, although it wasn't clear whether she meant you couldn't expect anything better of a man or of her sister. The child had to be dealt with, as they said in those days. Lucie was only twenty-one but she had already experienced this misfortune, and she was the one who found the "angel-maker" and organized the abortion, she also who made my aunt's shame less unbearable and her recovery easier.

But there was no doubting that Raphaëlle's heartbreak was overwhelming. She had lost a child, a lover, and the hope of a different life. "Yes, that was it, the thought of going to America made her happy..." my mother would say, furious that her sister had dared be happy. Raphaëlle was free, adventurous, flighty—all characteristics that she herself thought peculiar.

In spite of everything, the two girls' trajectories eventually met again in the late 1940s. Encouraged by their father, they started to sing. They modeled themselves on the Étienne Sisters, a swing duo who started out in the cabarets of Montmartre and whose glory days are now forgotten. Long before Yves Montand made his own recording of it, Odette and Louise Étienne had joined with Raymond Legrand's band and recorded *"C'est si bon"*:

C'est si bon
De partir n'importe où,
Bras dessus, bras dessous,
En chantant des chansons.

They also sang *"Plus je t'embrasse,"* a French adaptation of Ben Ryan's joyous ragtime number "Heart of My Heart," which dates from 1928 but is still in the repertoire of a few mechanical pianos and was covered by the Belgian singer Lio. As a child, I must have heard my mother sing-ing that song to herself a thousand times, and I know it by heart to this day: *"Le temps qui passe ne peut rien y changer..."*

It's no secret that Marceline dreamed that she and Raphaëlle would become the Michel Sisters. After all, having been born in a village in Meurthe-et-Moselle, they were no more provincial than their rivals from Reims. But here's the thing: Raphy "didn't want to work." They never performed to a proper audience and, already twenty-four, little Marceline fumed about this wasted opportunity: "You see," she would tell me, "what Raphaëlle wanted was to know how to sing before she'd learned." My more pragmatic aunt preferred to admit that neither one of them was a soprano. From what I've heard of the Étienne Sisters, singing well wasn't necessarily that important. In any event, two swing-singing sister duos was too much for the market.

1950. The elder sister was not exactly settled but had at least calmed down, and was dating Serge Bren-ner, a young engineer; the younger sister, now a woman, studied English, and the Serge Goupil she had met was a friend of Serge Brenner's. The two men shared more than a name and a diploma from Arts et Métiers in Paris: they both found their first jobs with the same employer, a French company that made earth-leveling machines, although my aunt's Serge was in sales and my future father in research. The similarities went further: one

Serge's parents lived on one side of rue Ordener and the other's on the opposite side.

A peculiarity: Serge Brenner had the same first name as his father, Serge Brenner. And when he and Raphaëlle had their first child, they baptized him Serge. This dynastic system was not at all practical: when my cousin, my uncle, and my great-uncle were all together, you couldn't call "Serge" without causing a degree of confusion.

Serge Brenner (the middle one, in this case) was taller, more effusive, and probably more on the ball than Serge Goupil. My future uncle was certainly quick to make a fortune: in scarcely ten years, my aunt and her whole family found themselves in a huge apartment in the Sixteenth Arrondissement of Paris, with two vast living rooms, a study, a guest room, and corridors as wide as rooms. You could play hide-and-seek in it, and a woman was employed full-time as a housekeeper.

My grandfather's illness was an opportunity for my mother to embark on competitive devotion for which, to be sure of greater success, she set down the rules. She insisted on driving him to the hospital for each transfusion. They were often very early in the morning, and Raphaëlle, who lived farther away and had to drop her children at school, was starting with a handicap. And when she did manage to free herself to take him, her younger sister would join them, unable to bear either being supplanted in this self-sacrifice or leaving her father alone with Raphaëlle. The latter eventually gave up. My mother never stopped reproaching her for this, while highlighting her own exemplary sacrifices. A remarkable case of selfish selflessness.

When her father died, Raphaëlle stopped the ritual vacations at the house in Picardie but started inviting her mother, her sister, my stepfather, and me to spend a week or two together as a family in the summer. It was often in a beautiful villa on the Côte d'Azur, in Cannes or Antibes, or a house in the very quaint Port-Grimaud. My uncle took us water-skiing in his speedboat, a Chris-Craft whose aggressive name fascinated me. This thirty-foot boat bore a very thinly disguised version of my cousin's name, *Lyna 1*. There was a *Lyna 2*, which was bigger, and a *Lyna 3*, which was faster. I didn't much care for this sport where I had to take off my thick-lensed glasses and face up to a hostile, unfocused world, and was happier staying on the deck enjoying the smack of the waves, the sea spray, and the roar of the engine.

In 1967, the Olympic skier Jean Vuarnet opened the ski resort of Avoriaz. It was revolutionary: a resort without cars, designed by a team of architects, accessible only by cable car, where you put on your skis at the door to your apartment building and traveled about the village in reindeer-drawn sleighs—it was Christmas all season. Sadly, the reindeer were gradually replaced with more efficient draft horses. The irregularly shaped buildings, all named after different conifers (Sequoia, larch, pine), were intended to blend with the mountains. My uncle bought a magnificent four-bedroom duplex very early on. He persuaded my mother and stepfather to invest there too. This was a major financial commitment for a couple of teachers, but they decided to buy a studio whose seasonal lettings almost covered the repayments. A good deal. We went for a couple of weeks in winter, having happy suppers every evening at my aunt and uncle's table before going home to our studio to sleep.

It was only later that I understood how much these holidays spent in luxury, thanks to her sister, exasperated and humiliated my mother. She may have been discreet in front of the whole family, but once alone with us she never stopped accusing her brother-in-law of taking kickbacks and making "shady deals," and—not without an element of self-contradiction—she criticized my father for being so honest or, worse still, for "lacking ambition"; in a word, for being "stupid." But it's difficult to be both an English teacher and in imports and exports.

My memories of Raphaëlle in those glory years are of a beautiful woman driving her Austin Mini too quickly, dividing her time between shopping, having her hair done, and her family. She was good-natured after a few drinks and, as there was always an open bottle of champagne in her fridge, she was always in a good mood. "I'm a little bit tipsy" was her catchphrase.

My mother, on the other hand, never drank. One drop of alcohol and she lost all self-control and succumbed to manic laughter, and the floodgates opened: she would say absolutely anything, an expression that usually means people say very specific things. The devil doesn't exist, which is exactly why he's so scary when he pops out of the box.

Sometimes, but not often enough, my aunt took me to the movies. I was thirteen when she took me to see Michel Boisrond's *On est toujours trop bon avec les femmes*, adapted from a book by Sally Mara, an alias of Raymond Queneau. The cast included the wonderful Jean-Pierre Marielle and the touching Élisabeth Wiener, and the music was by Claude Bolling. A whole different age, as they say. As we emerged from the dark auditorium, my aunt was still reeling from lines such as "I'll pin you like a butterfly," and kept saying I was too young for the film and she should never have taken me to see it. I couldn't see why.

In the early 1980s the stormy relationship between my aunt and uncle broke down. My aunt Raphaëlle, who had never had to work up to the age of fifty, opened her own business, a fashion boutique. She soon built up a clientele. My mother suddenly found they were on a more equal footing, strictly from a financial point of view.

Then my aunt met another man, a handsome old bachelor with long gray hair, older but no less wealthy than my uncle. He was high up in the dairy industry and clearly in love. She had always dreamed of America but had hardly set foot outside France: he made sure she traveled. They set off from Miami on a cruise in the Gulf of Mexico, stopping off along the coast of impoverished Central American countries. When she returned home and I was having lunch at her house, she took me to one side. I had been to Guatemala the previous year. Standing in her kitchen, she talked with some emotion about the huge market in Mérida, the capital of Yucatán, about the shocking disparity between tourists spilling out of steamboats and women in rags trying to sell them fruit and necklaces: "The people were so poor, you just can't imagine. Well, yes, you can imagine." She was genuinely disgusted by the cruelties of this world. Distressed and without artifice, she clutched my hands and kept saying, "I understand you, I understand you so well," as if my political commitments suddenly made sense to her. This was unsettling for the militant quasi-professional Trotskyist that I was at the time, and I couldn't think how to reply.

She went back into the dining room, sat down, and knocked back the rest of her glass of champagne. It was over. The destitute hoards were no longer mentioned in conversation, other than in anecdotal terms. But in that fleeting moment, her face had been colored not so much by pity as by sincere anger. All at once other people had existed, and she had seen herself right through to her heart; she had felt shame, the searing emotion that triggers morality and, in some cases, the fight. At the other end of the table, my mother sat watching her sister blankly. Had she ever felt ashamed? If I'd asked her the question she'd have shaken her head and replied, "Ashamed of what?"

The years went by. Raphaëlle separated again. She stopped traveling and, now suffering another reversal of fortune, she turned to her sister: Guy had just inherited some money. As in the fable about the ant and the grasshopper, the newly rich ant could at this point have laughed at the fallen grasshopper, but the pleasure of being in a position to help Raphaëlle was even more powerful. My mother helped her as if handing back change. My aunt sold her fur coats, and my mother also bought Chinese ivory vases from her, even though she didn't like them. Raphaëlle's former glory was changing hands. And the age-old tensions between the rival sisters seemed to fade.

But after Guy died, not a week went by without my mother descending into a period of dementia whose first manifestation was a peculiar fabrication: she convinced herself that, until Guy's dying day, her sister had been his mistress. And overnight her husband became a "bastard" and her sister most definitely a "whore."

"I hate her!" she would shriek, walking up the street and calling the whole world to witness. "Don't you see, don't you see!" she'd rail at me, "what a bunch of sleazeballs!"

The idea was so improbable that no one could share in her madness, and this general incredulity only aggravated her fury.

Nothing stacked up.

First there was the simple question of scheduling. An adulterous relationship, however poor quality it is, takes time. Now, my mother and Guy rarely left each other's side. If he went out, it was for an hour at the most. I would guess that my aunt, with her lust for life, would have struggled to settle for so little.

But the main thing with adultery is that there need to be two people, and I couldn't imagine what Raphaëlle would have seen in Guy, who was definitely neither handsome, funny, clever, nor charming. A study of the men she had chosen to have by her side through life left no hope for the Guy hypothesis.

My mother came up with a new fabrication every day: my cousin had allegedly "confirmed" the affair, then it was a "friend" whose name she'd forgotten but who had caught them together, years earlier, in the "back room of the shop," or even her sister herself had "confessed everything."

She took to Scotch-taping dozens of notes, envelopes, and advertising leaflets to the walls of her apartment. She wrote: "I don't want Raphy THE WHORE at my funeral. I CURSE HER!" capitals included. Luckily, my mother was not on Twitter.

She once told me she always carried a kitchen knife on her. "In case I see Raphy." I searched her handbag. It wasn't true.

My cousin told me that the two women did bump into each other in the street once. Confronted with my mother's accusations, Raphaëlle had shaken her head in bafflement.

"Well then swear to me, I mean *swear* to me," my mother said, "that you never slept with Guy."

"I swear it," said my aunt.

"Swear it on our father's grave, and I'll believe you," my mother insisted.

"I swear on our father's grave," said my aunt.

There was a long silence, then my mother spat out, "I don't believe you."

She walked off briskly, furious, leaving a dumbstruck Raphaëlle alone on the boulevard.

This meant my mother had killed two birds with one stone: she never had to go visit the grave of her bastard of a husband, and she'd found what she thought was the best excuse not to see her whore of a sister.

But every vocational victim does need an original torturer. And that was my father.

· SEVEN ·

BEGETTER

*In the absence of more precise
information, no one, starting with
me, knew what the hell I was
doing here on earth.*

JEAN-PAUL SARTRE, *LES MOTS*

M y mother has described the first episode in my
life at which my father was present: she and he
are in the kitchen of the one-bedroom apart-
ment on rue Baudelique, near the *Mairie* of the Eighteenth
Arrondissement.

"I'd so love to have a child," my father said suddenly,
as if emerging from a dream.

"But...you have a son, he's right here," said my mother,
indicating me, a pink six-month-old baby having his bottle.

I don't know to this day whether the scene contains
even a small element of truth or my mother invented every
aspect of it—either way, she repeated it endlessly, in the
undisguised hope of breaking me away from my father. I
tend toward the first hypothesis, even though my mother

used the same wording too many times for the episode not to have been somewhat embroidered.

My first true memory of him is a photo: a small Paris dining room that looked out over the very Modiano-like rue Ordener, and where almost the entire room is filled by a table covered with an oilcloth. There are the leftovers of dessert, crumbs from an epiphany cake. I've forgotten whether I was allowed to have the lucky charm from the cake. On the far side of the table, a man stands leaning against a tall dresser filled with ornamental plates; he is cautiously, anxiously watching a boy of seven or eight, who doesn't look any more at home in this slightly suffocating space. It's a compulsory get-together, on a Sunday, at my paternal grandparents' house, a sort of failed father-son speed date. He hasn't dared come closer to me on this particular occasion, and I have no memory of tender gestures in any of our subsequent "dates," ever. In his defense, I did get the feeling he was holding them back, that he'd allowed too much distance to grow between us and now couldn't cover it in the few scant hours we saw each other, unless he was paralyzed by some notion of "betraying" my mother. This is the only memory I have of my paternal grandparents' apartment, which I visited very little. The place has now accumulated plenty of other, more painful memories because, by a miracle of urban regeneration, it has become my dentist's office. Lacanists would say I go there to have my aches and twinges treated. I'm not so sure, though.

Because my father was not really the paternal sort. At the very least, his expertise in that area was limited.

My begetter was only twenty-two when he met my mother, who was just twenty. She was his first, and he hers. Two years later, when neither of them had finished their studies, they were married.

Serge and Marceline lived together for seven years, in that little place on rue Baudelique. I was born late in the equation, probably at the most inopportune moment. My father had just met another woman, Marinette, and she was very likely already his mistress when I was conceived. Perhaps my mother, intuiting the infidelity, hoped this would be a way to keep my father? I don't know much about Marinette, apart from her name and the fact—which is, to say the least, a cliché—that she was his secretary.

My mother must have been sufficiently suspicious to rifle through Serge's jacket regularly in search of signs, or even proof, of the affair. She eventually found what she was looking for and, when he came home from work one evening, my father found his suitcases out on the landing and a new lock on the door that none of his keys would open. My grandfather had sent in a locksmith. My father had to take refuge with his parents, then his sister, and the little apartment stood empty for a few weeks because my mother and I were taken in by her parents.

My father called every day, several times a day, but my mother refused to speak to him, an extremely radical stance for a woman who accommodated so many other things in the world. It was my grandmother who picked up and explained to him that, at least for a while, he mustn't keep trying to get hold of Marceline. She was so hurt. He then agreed, without undue heartache, to disappear from my mother's life and mine. Grandpa negotiated the terms, "for my sake." He did it with a patriarchal authority that no one had ever dared contest, and not without nerve, because he was hardly an authority on the subject of conjugal fidelity.

It was only when I became a father myself that I realized two stray planets had collided all those years ago: a perpetual victim drunk on revenge and a man relieved to be released from his responsibilities as a father.

I don't know how many months or years his affair with Marinette lasted. I know so little about his life. I knew of only two other women: Svetlana, then Rosy.

My father met Svetlana in 1967, when he was on a business trip to Prague. Back then, when Czechoslovakia was part of the now atomized Soviet bloc, no one could have envisaged negotiating in the despised English language, although both sides of the table mastered it. So Svetlana was the pretty, ubiquitous interpreter. She was twenty-three, he forty, she had blue eyes, he a blue passport: they were made to get along. Despite her young age, she had—besides her urgent desire to cross the iron curtain—two sons, Marek and Radim: she had left a terrible husband who, she admitted to Serge, used to beat her.

Hopelessly in love, Serge went to see her two or three times before marrying her, on a final trip to Prague. Back in Paris he made all the necessary arrangements. Particularly as Svetlana was now pregnant, with a girl, my future half sister. In order to have her baby in France, she soon joined him with her two children. Her naturalization appears to have been accelerated.

Sadly, the now French Svetlana seemed less smitten with Serge than the Czech Svetlana had been, and the idyll swiftly descended into fistfights. When Valérie was born, the relationship was already more than a little shaky. Serge didn't get along with the two boys, whom I met only once and who struck me as stubborn and brimming over with violence. All the same, in a letter to my mother from that period, he said he wanted to "love them like his own children," which—and I say this with no malice intended— didn't commit him to very much. But he never had the opportunity to express these brand-new paternal feelings because Svetlana separated from him shortly afterward, accusing him of domestic violence, which he always denied. She secured a ruling from the remarkably obliging judge, that their little daughter should stay with Serge.

Serge would discover later that, for some years, she had been in a relationship with the notary who had drawn up the terms of their marriage. This man dealt still more diligently with their divorce proceedings. Svetlana left my father with a little girl he didn't really know what to do with and another alimony to pay. Then, abandoning the notary to his work, she set sail for Corsica with her two boys and, rather extravagantly, opened a Thai restaurant in Porto-Vecchio. She remarried, had two daughters this time, then divorced again. The woman had energy to burn.

I saw Serge only on very rare occasions, and these never coincided with Christmas or my birthday. He was invited to my First Communion, I'm sure of it, and I think I glimpsed him at my mother's fortieth birthday the following year.

Along came the year of my baccalaureate, which I passed without particular distinction. I hadn't seen my father for four years, and he invited me to celebrate my success in a touristy restaurant on the place du Tertre. For many years, his own father had been a hobby painter in Montmartre, and I still have some paintings by this Goupil grandfather, including an attractive street scene of the rue des Saules and a fairly decent candlelit still life. I remember nothing about that lunch, except that we sat in full sunlight, I ate a large rare steak au poivre, and for two hours I evaded the question of nomenclature: Should I call him Dad? Or just Serge? We were about to say our goodbyes when a scissor artist offered to cut my profile out of card. Serge accepted and I sat down on the stool, for too long; I wanted to go, wanted this slightly pointless father-son thing to be over as soon as possible. The portrait was finished at last. I thought Serge wanted to keep it as a memento of his lunch with his son, but no, he offered it to me: it was quite a good likeness. We went our separate ways, and I walked home, accelerated by the steep slope and a less heavy heart, holding this flat black sort of replica of myself. I wanted to throw the cutout away, but some part of me refused to end up in the trash. I kept it.

On July 5, 1974, President Valéry Giscard d'Estaing reduced the age of majority in France to eighteen. This meant that I became an adult some three months later: I left my family home two days after my birthday. A friend put me up, but a quick calculation told me my savings wouldn't last long. I made up my mind to call Serge. I briefly explained my new status as a math student without a bean to his name. He listened in silence.

Sadly, things were "tricky" right now, it was "bad timing."

He and Svetlana were getting divorced in the worst circumstances for him. And anyway, he couldn't see why, even though I'd left home, "my parents" refused to support me. Particularly as, by abandoning his name for my stepfather's, I had chosen a "symbolic break from my line of descent." I regretted asking for help; I even apologized. I'm one of those people you can knock into in the street and they say sorry. We both had the same sense of relief when we ended the call.

Years went by. I thought I'd seen him definitively eclipsed from my life when I received a call from him, right at the end of the seventies. The conversation started strangely. First, he told me about his recent promotion in his new company, then mentioned meeting Rosy, a tall, slim blonde who was a "model." He couldn't get over how they'd met: a minor fender-bender, which meant they'd had to exchange telephone numbers (he had been at fault). They were getting married the following week, and I grasped from reading between the lines that it was his future wife who wanted me to be part of the scenery for the nuptial event. Sadly, I replied, things were "tricky" right now, it was "bad timing." I take no pride in this retort, it was all that came to me.

I did, however, accept the next invitation. I'd never met Valérie, who was thirteen, and Sonia, my companion, accompanied me. She was a math student like me, but a far more brilliant one, and many years later, by chance, she became Jacques Roubaud's assistant. Back in Paris after the outing, Sonia criticized me for being too sarcastic; she felt I'd pulled the wool over everyone's eyes, hidden my true emotions. I don't remember now.

My most enduring memory of that day is a long time spent in the bathroom. Serge had invented a "pressure-operated magazine for submarine crossbows" and had patented it in the United States (US 4496641 7 A); he was testing it out in his bathtub. Since being made redundant, he made use of the enforced leisure time. The world also had him to thank for a "transverse leveling device for parked trailers (particularly caravans)" (patent EP 0011029 AI), and an "adjustable insulating sunscreen" (patent EP 0031592 AI). Not forgetting the "paternal relations concealment system" that he hadn't thought to patent.

More time passed. I abandoned mathematics and started studying journalism. One day, the phone rang and a woman's voice said, "Hello, Hervé, it's your sister."

"My sister? But I don't have a sister," I said without a moment's hesitation.

There was a long silence.

"But you do, you do," the voice said eventually, overcoming its disappointment. "I'm Valérie, your sister."

Valérie was now fifteen, I was still eight years older, and she wanted to invite this big brother she'd met only once to her birthday. I felt ashamed and went along on a rainy Sunday in November. It was ghastly: there was an hour of peace, then everything descended into what must have been their everyday life. Rosy fought with the hypersensitive teenager, calling her insolent, and Serge—visibly tired of living with a daughter he found "difficult"—couldn't manage even a modicum of patience. Valérie was completely strung out, and she cried with helpless rage when the time came for the cake. Ten months later she fled to her mother, who probably didn't want to be burdened with her too much either. But at least in Corsica there was the fragrant scrubland and the sunshine.

Another few years. At my mother's request, I organized a "family" party at my apartment for my thirtieth birthday; she also insisted I invite Serge. From the first couple of words they exchanged, it became clear that for my mother this was mostly about giving Serge an opportunity to gauge my social advancement, as she wandered around the large Paris apartment that my income as a young editor meant I could afford. As she demonstrated to Serge just how far I'd outstripped him, my mother savored the triumph. She drank half a glass of wine and succumbed to one of her bouts of uncontrollable manic laughter, and it held her in its grips for a good twenty minutes, to the extent that her husband started worrying about her hiccups. Then, when the time came for dessert, Serge felt very faint and had to lie down. I called the emergency services. Whichever way you looked at it, the evening was a success.

I then had no news of him at all for twenty years. But I did come across my half sister once, at Porto-Vecchio, where I was having a vacation. By then a nurse's aide in Ajaccio, she was married to a baker, a hard-bitten Corsican separatist but such a taciturn man I don't know anything else about him. We had dinner in a nondescript restaurant and an atmosphere of relative tension because he leaned against the wall and kept one eye on the door as if afraid armed men might burst in at any moment. Serge was our main topic of conversation. Having spent a great deal of time with him, Valérie clearly had much more to complain about than I did.

I often regret these missed opportunities between my half sister and me. No one finds it easy escaping the fantasy of family, and a relationship with Valérie—even a distant one built ex nihilo—would have been the closest I could get to that. But I have too little experience of blood ties, and I have to admit I was wary of the Sacred Alliance of orphans.

Twenty years went by, and then it was Rosy who called me. She wanted me to come to Serge's eightieth birthday. She said it would be a "surprise." I enlisted my son Melville, on the brink of adolescence, to come with me. I wanted him to put a face to this very absent grandfather. And, after all, it might be his only and last opportunity to meet one quarter of his genetic inheritance. Valérie was there, with her children; her daughter was the same age as my son, and Melville had an unusual but enjoyable day. Serge was surrounded by very close friends who were astonished to discover he had a son and even a grandson. For my part, I have to acknowledge that I was happy to see him, especially as he was in very good shape, which went some way to reassuring me about my medical future.

It was the last time we saw each other, though. He died two years later. But mortals can't help living with magical thinking and for me, his funeral was our real last meeting, and the most straightforward too.

I went with my partner, my son, my mother and my aunt, and Guy. My half sister cried; her children held her hands, dry-eyed: they'd seen so little of their grandfather. Svetlana was not there.

I was standing slightly apart from the small crowd of friends in the cemetery when I noticed an old man watching me. He took a step toward me.

"You're Serge's son, aren't you?"

I nodded.

"You stand the way he did, you know. Posture, eh?"

"No, I didn't know. I didn't know him very well."

"What a shame! My condolences, anyway."

The man walked away, and a woman came over to me.

"You *are* Serge's son, aren't you?"

"Yes."

"You stand very upright, just like him. You have the same outline."

"Really? I wouldn't know. We never saw each other."

"How sad for a father not to see his son!"

I smiled, slightly disarmed. A third person came up to me. To cut short any conversation, I pretended to pick up my cell phone, and walked a few paces away. I wonder whether Serge held his phone in exactly the same way.

In my pocket I had that cut-out portrait of my silhouette made some forty years earlier. I was planning to throw it into his grave, along with a white rose. Once again, I kept it.

EIGHT

GUY

He's a lad of no importance collectively,
he's quite simply an individual.
LOUIS-FERDINAND CÉLINE, *L'ÉGLISE*

I'm not sure how to talk about Guy. Well, at first I called him "Daddy Guy," then simply "Daddy"— three syllables were far too many to express the degree of affection and simply weren't practical for everyday use. "Daddy" was not only easier but also legitimate, given that the only genetically qualified pretender, "Daddy Serge," had gradually absented himself and could no longer really lay claim to the title. I don't remember ever using the argument, during a fight, that Guy "wasn't my father." It would have felt all the more unfair because I would also have rejected a "true" father's authority anyway.

I don't know under what circumstances he appeared in my mother's life and, to be brutally honest, I've never felt any curiosity on the subject. They say children often ask their parents questions. Daddy, how did you meet

Mommy? I've never been interested in that. Perhaps this indifference was simply my form of resistance. As my Goupil begetter had voluntarily stepped out of the picture and I would never truly belong to the aristocratic Le Tellier dynasty, dreaming up a creation story for myself wouldn't have offered even the beginnings of a solution.

An only son, the last offshoot of a waning aristocratic strain, pampered and adulated by his mother, Guy had consistently failed in his studies and had no qualifications to his name when he met my very newly divorced mother. How he managed to seduce her remains a mystery to me. He probably made the most of a favorable window when her pain at the separation was giving way to a longing for revenge—definitely against Serge and perhaps also against all men. This new marriage was her first form of vengeance.

One thing is sure: my mother took Guy in hand. He joined her in England and improved his English—and there was a great deal of room for improvement; then she urged him to start studying again. The previously mediocre student secured a degree—not without difficulty—and became a teacher, first at junior high school level. His English accent and vocabulary tended to ossify during these years spent teaching, but what with favorable inspection reports and accumulated seniority, he eventually qualified as a high school teacher.

My mother had complete authority over him. He was visibly afraid of her fits of rage, which were both terrifying and unpredictable, and he had abdicated any form of resistance. She made all the decisions, and she had such a hold over him that she even composed the letters he wrote to his family. He simply had to copy out her rough drafts. At the end of these letters my mother even added the name "Guy" so he didn't forget to sign them.

Authority. Guy never fought for it. His day-to-day existence was a buildup of chores and submissive acceptances that were never reevaluated or even questioned. He had been a Boy Scout for a long time, a simple setup where the world was what it was. *Being a Scout,* claimed a manual from 1937, meant *Serving, Believing, Obeying the law, Bringing boys together and Working hard.* Quite a program. In response to my ubiquitous "Whys?" he preferred to reply with a servile "That's the way it is" rather than an "I don't know," which would at least have led the way to searching for an answer.

If the world is divided into two types (those who think the earth revolves around the sun and the rest; those who like dodecaphonic music and the rest, etc.), and this is of course a simplistic dichotomy, I'm one of the people who think parents have duties toward their children, and Guy is one of those who conversely think children have duties toward their parents. One of these duties was never to judge them in any way. I was, in this respect at least, a poor example.

If I criticized my mother he was immediately furious and would wail indignantly, "How dare you talk about your mother like that?"

My reply might be something like, "What if I were Hitler's son, should I keep my mouth shut then too?"

I admit that, having always enjoyed pushing an argument to its limits to test its validity, I quickly reached the Godwin point, that *reductio ad hitlerum* which means you can counter anti-tobacco campaigners with, "Oh, I see, so you agree with Hitler, do you?"

"Are you comparing your mother to Hitler?" my step-father would then splutter, a response I'd anticipated and therefore wanted.

I'd have been so much happier if he'd said, "Don't speak ill of the Führer, my boy."

But irony wasn't his strongest suit, and his anger did not represent intelligently considered antifascism. It simply endorsed the now generally held view that Hitler was the personification of evil.

This submission to prevalent thinking had a counterpart: barely restrained violence that I could sense and feared as a child. He was an ordered man, incapable of disrupting his habits, and—even if confronted with his own mistakes—incapable of changing his opinion. The word "intransigent" could have been invented for him.

His daily life was punctuated by immutable rituals.

Guy woke early and silently every morning and did his exercises for precisely twenty minutes. This iron discipline had not granted him an athlete's body. He had drooping shoulders despite the push-ups, his legs remained skinny despite the repetitions, and his torso had thickened rather than grown broader. Next he showered and then shaved. His shaving routine took ten minutes: he wore an impeccably well-tended Third Republic goatee. His tool of choice was a safety razor with a double-edged replaceable blade, an implement that dated from his teenage years and was invented by King Camp Gillette in 1895. In fact, it was already so outdated in the seventies that Georges Perec could have included it in his book *I Remember*. The day came when the pharmacist warned Guy that production of the blades would soon stop. Guy ordered enough for a century of whiskers.

Later, when I was drawing up an inventory of his quirks, I realized that he was submerged by what psychiatry calls obsessive-compulsive behaviors.

Guy always wore a necktie. On the face of it—and I say this to reassure tie-wearing readers—you can't draw any conclusions from that. Particularly as it was a simple, ordinary-looking silk tie, not too thin or casual, not knitted or too bold because he wouldn't have known what to wear with it. His tie was almost always single-colored, usually in the dark blue range, but occasionally it might be broken up by a thin stripe. I gave him ties in different colors or with novelty designs, but in vain. They ended up at the bottom of a drawer, at the very best. The others, some fifty of them, hung on a long double metal hanger in his wardrobe, and I'd have struggled to distinguish them from each other.

His preferred tying method was a straightforward knot. It wasn't a Windsor knot whose width suits Italian collars, or a half-Windsor invented for narrow ties, nor the elegant crossed Christensen knot, which doesn't cope well with thicker silks, not to mention the Onassis, which sets you apart from the crowd at a party, but what party would that be? Mustn't let our imagination get away with us. If pushed, my stepfather could tie a Prince Albert, feeding the loose end around twice, but this alone was a wild eccentricity for him.

He was too short in the trunk and not thick enough in the neck, and he chose ties that were too long. However fastidiously he tucked the ends into his pants, they always came free eventually, and flapped out of control over his belt buckle.

I don't know how he acquired his taste for this decorative strip of cloth. Teaching English at high school level hardly required him to wear one. I imagine it was an unconscious effort on his part to establish an insurmountable sort of sartorial Maginot line between him and his pupils. Unless other meanings of the word "tie"—a link, a connection, something that binds—were the key to any analysis. Either way, once home he never took the thing off or even loosened his collar. For a long time, I believed he simply couldn't be bothered. Along came retirement, though, and still he wore a tie. He tied it every morning, whatever the weather and whatever was going on. He wore it indiscriminately under a suit, a sweater, a jacket, or an anorak, and all this conspired to make him look like a guard who worked for a security firm. His bad knees meant he couldn't ski but he sometimes took my son up the mountains, and he wore his tie right to the foot of the ski runs. He could even wear a tie to eat fondue in a mountaintop restaurant—I have the picture to prove it. It must have been a wrench taking the thing off to sleep or bathe.

His conformity was so extreme it bordered on originality.

Another point: Guy hurried slowly.

Festina lente, some Ancients said, and the Medicis made it their motto. But he was so slow it was exasperating. I noticed it only when it came into conflict with my childish impatience, and that happened a lot. Setting off for a vacation was a prime example. An airline pilot checking every instrument in the cockpit could learn a thing or two from him: Guy checked everything at least twice, from closing the windows to shutting off the gas supply, from switching off the meter to double-locking the doors. Sometimes we'd finally be sitting in the car and he'd go back up to check one last time that the door really was shut, and it took so long that I suspect he used the opportunity to have another look at the windows, the gas, the meter, etc.

Then the time came to load the suitcases. The trunk of a car is usually basically a parallelepiped, and the trunk of the Ami 6 station wagon that my parents acquired in 1965, shortly after its launch, did not deviate from the norm. The number of suitcases that needed packing into it could be counted on the fingers of one hand, and loading a station wagon requires no special talent, but it could take him a half hour. When, as a child, he had to put all the cubes and cylinders in the appropriate slots in kindergarten, his teacher must frequently have had a weary note in her voice as night fell and she told him, "That's very good, Guy. But you can finish it tomorrow."

At last we would set off, but only after his seat had been adjusted to within a millimeter, and the side mirrors repositioned. Getting out of a parking space took him longer than it would have taken anyone else to get into it. At the first traffic lights he would stop, despite the light being green, in order to avoid going through an amber light. And the light could never switch to green without the car behind us honking at least once.

A classic phobic obsession: Guy also cleaned constantly. He never stopped sponging, polishing, and rubbing. The kitchen gleamed as it had on the day it was installed. As a teenager, I ended up viewing this particular behavioral disorder with detachment, even making it something of a game. I would sometimes put a bread crumb on the polished marble worktop to see how long it survived. A few seconds at best, as long as it took to be spotted. This was a distraction, for a while.

There was also his medication. Everyone has a medicine cabinet; Guy on the other hand had a medicine *closet*. It's a question of scale. I won't deny that he must have had a cardiac complaint, but his hypochondria demanded respect, so much so that I sometimes think he had his triple bypass and his pacemaker only as precautionary measures. He tended to a negligible cholesterol problem, nonthreatening diabetes, and tachycardia that hadn't put in an appearance for ten years, and he gorged himself on antibiotics at the slightest cold. Capsules and pills were lined up at the beginning and end of every meal, and the best present I ever gave him was a pill container. When, at age sixty, he came into money, he could indulge his passion for doctors' appointments. Once when I had a problem with breathlessness, I took his advice and made an appointment with his cardiologist, a "big shot." You could have held a prom in the man's waiting room, where I sat alone, and I definitely think the thing on the wall was a Bram van Velde. The specialist examined me, took an electrocardiogram, concluded it was due to a bit of stress, and advised me to do more walking. He told me to say hello to my stepfather and to remind him of his appointment that Friday, because they saw each other twice a month. Then he told me what the consultation had cost:

five days' work at minimum wage. He wanted to see me again for further tests. I thanked him for his concern, but I'd call back. I'm still alive as I write.

But I don't want to be too hard on Guy. It's the way he was, that's all.

.

. .

Correction: that may be the way he was, but he hadn't always been like that. He'd had a happy childhood and was a boisterous teenager. He still liked talking about his years as the class dunce at the very bourgeois Janson-de-Sailly high school, about student parades and carousing, even if his worst prank didn't go beyond ringing doorbells. He even described having been briefly, and against all probability, a "socialist student." He was also a monitor at Claude-Bernard high school in the fifties, and when I read a biography of Georges Perec I discovered that my future stepfather must have overseen the future author and member of Oulipo. But the name Georges Perec meant nothing to him, not as a schoolboy or a poet.

In his last years, chance brought him together with André Val, an old friend from Janson high school with whom he'd lost touch. André was tall and slim with a deep, peculiarly lilting voice. He had married a very Catholic and very reactionary woman whose shyness single-handedly spared the two friends from her stupidity. Guy and André didn't see much of each other, but on each occasion André's domineering and often ironic tone of voice implied that he'd essentially been a bigger, stronger boy and, having tormented Guy in the past, he was slipping straight back into the role of torturer. He took pleasure in reminding Guy of countless past humiliations, and invented new ones better suited to their advancing years; Guy meanwhile submitted to this. I found it painful that, perfectly illustrating Stockholm syndrome, my stepfather enjoyed André's company.

One time when André had steered the conversation onto the subject of sex and Guy had been bold enough to follow him, he spat out a "Don't tell me you can still get it up! Marceline, we want proof. Proof!"

Guy couldn't find the right rejoinder—when a gentle "Why don't you ask your wife?" would have been enough. And my mother laughed, overcome with embarrassment, before succumbing to a fit of manic laughter that was still more embarrassing for the rest of us.

Mind you, Guy had suffered a mortification—this one chocolate-related—on his very first date with my mother. He had given her a box of heart-shaped praline truffles. The box was also heart-shaped. It was too sentimental: she found it "totally ridiculous," threw the box on the ground and trampled on it. "And here is my heart which beats for you alone," Verlaine wrote. My mother tore it up with her two white feet.

I can't imagine Guy as he was before meeting my mother. A spark had gone out, for sure. Chamfort says it's better to be a lesser thing but be true to yourself. I've often thought that Guy neither wanted to be more, nor managed to be himself. It wasn't a failure. He was fired by no ambition, not even to live.

They must have known happy years, even—let's risk using the word—love, but I have no proof of this: I never saw my mother demonstrate a jot of affection for him, or even make a tender gesture toward him. And sometimes a deep wave of cruelty could spring up in her.

They were in Deauville for a long weekend. Guy had to return to Paris by train to sit for some exams, and she went to see him off at the station. A thin, greasy slice of *saucisson* had slipped from someone's sandwich and was awaiting its victim. As he walked, Guy put the heel of his shoe squarely on it and, there in the station concourse, executed a tumble worthy of Captain Haddock at Marlinspike Hall. He fell heavily. People around him came to help him solicitously, but my mother was laughing so hard she had to sit down, and between her hiccups she just kept saying, "I'm sorry, Guy, but really, *really*! How stupid can you get!" In spite of everything he caught his train with dignity, a cracked coccyx, and what turned out to be quite a sprain. Years later, she would still describe this scene in front of an embarrassed Guy, who opted to smile about it.

The last memory I have of their relationship before he went into the hospital and never came out again, was a short visit to the country. I joined them there, afraid they might throw out my furniture during a sort of inventory of the barn that they were carrying out with the gardener and his wife, who looked after the house.

In the barn was an old Pathé-Marconi radio—cum—record player, a large piece with lights and mica condensers. It dated back to the days of swing and cha-cha-cha but still worked if you gave the bulbs long enough to warm up.

"My parents gave it to me for my twentieth birthday," Guy said and, looking emotional, he added with a sigh, "My, do I have some memories of this."

This was too much for my mother, who barked angrily and contemptuously, "Memories, memories! Well, thanks! I'll give you some brand-new memories!"

This completely unpredictable explosion startled even the phlegmatic gardener, and Guy stared at my mother in astonishment.

"Come on, scram, scram!" she kept saying.

My stepfather wouldn't have been able to save the record player from the landfill site and destruction. It's to me—who expressed an interest in the piece and had to fight long and hard—that he owes its survival.

Under the Pathé-Marconi emblem are the words: "His Master's Voice."

I'll give it to whoever wants it.

NINE

LA MAISON LE TELLIER

War in castles! Peace in cottages!
DECREE OF DECEMBER 15, 1792

The aristocratic legend of my stepfather's family has it that the Le Telliers were directly descended from William the Conqueror. The prospect that the Queen of England could, as it were, be her vassal made my mother puff herself up with an absurd enthusiasm that already embarrassed me as a child.

For Elizabeth II to have the privilege of kneeling before my mother, the latter would of course first have to accede to the rank of a Le Tellier, a potential promotion that must have carried considerable weight in her choice of this otherwise fairly insubstantial husband. But, in the bosom of that aristocratic family, her status as a divorced woman with a child made her an incongruous import. My mother was therefore never accepted, and her offspring enjoyed little more success.

Time for an aside: the Le Telliers were actually descended from one Michel Le Tellier, a clever middle-class fellow, admittedly a Norman, whom Louis XIII appointed as secretary of state and Louis XIV made the Marquis of Barbezieux, Lord of Chaville, Étang, and Viroflay. More important, the Sun King appointed his son, François Michel, secretary of state for war and gave him the title of Marquis of Louvois, having given him the Château de Louvois as a wedding gift. The coat of arms was rather elegant, in azure with three silver lizards one above the other, surmounted by three gold stars.

Unfortunately, Louvois is best known for signing the abrogation of the Edict of Nantes, in 1685, having carried out many intimidating *dragonnades*, forcing Huguenots to convert to Catholicism. To please the church, Louis XIV had that same year brought an end to state arbitration, and had persecuted Jews, Huguenots, and Jansenists, causing hordes of them to flee the country. It was a terrible retrograde step for France, the country's worst drain of economic, intellectual, and social capital.

As a teenager, I was distraught to find my family name in *Les Misérables*, that defense of the Revolution's brutality against the barbarity of the ancien régime. Through the strong but gentle voice of the dying conformist G., Hugo wrote:

> *The elder Duchêne is ferocious, but what epithet will you furnish me for the elder Letellier? Jourdan-Coupe-Tête*

is a monster, but less than the Marquis de Louvois. Monsieur,
monsieur, I mourn Marie Antoinette, archduchess and queen,
but I also mourn that poor Huguenot woman who, in 1685,
under Louis le Grand, monsieur, while nursing her child,
was stripped to the waist and tied to a post, while her child
was held before her; her breast swelled with milk and her
heart with anguish; the baby, weak and famished, seeing the
breast, cried in agony; and the executioner said to the nursing
mother, "Recant!" giving her the choice between the death of her
child and the death of her conscience. What do you say to this
Tantalus torture inflicted on a mother?

Reading that gave some perspective to any pride I had in bearing the name.

End of the aside.

Although I called Guy "Daddy," I don't remember treating his father to "Grandfather," "Grandad," or other "Grandpa" terms, and I'm sure I never knew how to address his mother. She displayed no animosity toward me, but I sensed that coming out with a "Granny" would have been totally absurd and would have made her shudder with dread. I probably circumvented the problem in my own way when we visited them while they just called me Hervé, which was easy.

It was my stepfather's maternal family, the Sainte-Lucies, who rejected my mother the most. "Etiolated and in-bred," she retorted, but with less scorn than jealousy. But, on closer inspection, the subject is more complex.

The Sainte-Lucies were first and foremost three sisters—Simone, Yvette, and Odette—born at intervals of twelve months. Yvette was my stepfather's mother. Simone, the eldest, was his godmother, "Godmother Mone"; and Odette the youngest. Their age difference wasn't at all obvious to me.

My mother loathed Godmother Mone.

"She really thinks she's something, that one."

This was most likely true, but I had few sources of information or contradictory analyses. Be that as it may, I ended up seeing this woman as a sort of wicked fairy godmother, both haughty and malevolent. Simone had never married ("Well, who would want her?" my mother jeered), had a responsible position at the *Mairie* ("She got that by pulling strings"), and had been in the Resistance ("Hah! No one's ever seen any proof…"). Still, in the seventies Godmother Mone took to proudly wearing the rosette of the Légion d'honneur, a reward landed very late in the day, it has to be said, for an active member of some clandestine network. But I'm no expert.

The youngest, Odette, married an Odet, which could have demonstrated a lack of originality if the man hadn't had perfectly black skin. So I had a Great-Uncle Odet— my Tont'Odet—with jet black coloring, a lean frame, and a handsome, lined face, and who was always "all spruced up," as my mother used to say. Originally from Guadeloupe but not mixed race, he was a lawyer at the Paris bar, known and respected by his peers, and he had asked for Odette's hand in the 1930s. He had been granted it with no hesitation, and not one of the Sainte-Lucies had ever uttered any reticence about the advent of a man of color in the family. He would often playfully tell the story of his wedding night, when he stepped out of the shower with his tightly curled hair wet and unruly, finally freed of its coating of brilliantine, and his young wife took fright at the sight and realized for the first time that she had married a Maasai warrior.

Tont'Odet even told me he'd lived his life without ever really coming across racism. I found this hard to believe until the day when, aged eighty, he came home from a café on the place de L'Opéra deeply shaken. While he'd been drinking his coffee a "hoodlum" had called him a "nigger." He'd struck the man with his walking stick, seen him off, and—shaking with indignation—stood on the sidewalk and launched into a long speech in defense of France and its republican values. The crowd, he said with some emotion and a hint of pride, had cheered and clapped. It was perfectly possible.

Nevertheless, he was obsessed with black culture. He devoted years to researching the life of Chevalier de Saint-George. There's no denying it was an extraordinary life:

Joseph Boulogne de Saint-George was born a slave in about 1745, the son of a colonist and a black slave woman. He arrived in Bordeaux when he was very young and although he was mixed race, his teenage years were spent like a young French aristocrat and he went on to pursue a double career as a violin virtuoso and an extraordinarily talented fencer: a painting by Robineau bears witness to a friendly bout with Chevalier d'Éon at Carlton House, before a select audience drawn from the English nobility. Better still, having enjoyed the protection of the Orléans for a long time, Saint-George had rallied behind the Revolution, committed to the antislavery movement, and founded the *Légion franche des Américains*, a mounted unit comprising men of color and committed to the newly formed republic…until this republic disappointed him with its fatal Napoleonic stalemate. He was a character with an unusual trajectory, a cosmopolitan adventurer who couldn't fail to fascinate a man such as Odet.

Tont'Odet showed me genuine affection and when he took me for walks—often to the Vincennes Zoological Gardens—I was proud to walk beside this man who was so black and so elegant, and who, when we stopped off in a bistro, delighted in saying, "Waiter, a little black one for me and a hot chocolate for my big nephew."

I was twenty-five when he gave me his last book, a small volume published by such a little-known company that he must have paid for it himself. I struggled somewhat to get through it: he candidly described his childhood and his professional and family life, and I'm sure there was the word "humanism" in the title.

My stepfather cherished him, and when I cast about for reasons to respect Guy, or even like him, it was in that sincerely felt affection that I sought them.

I remember very little of Yvette, whom my stepfather called "Mamour." She was a housewife, a self-effacing woman of utmost discretion, almost invisible. But inaudible she certainly was not. On the rare Sundays when we visited, she often ended up leaning on the grand piano in the living room, singing the "Flower Duet" from *Lakmé* with her sister Odette, accompanied by her son.

Sous le dôme épais où le blanc jasmin
À la rose s'assemble,
Sur la rive en fleurs, riant au matin,
Viens, descendons ensemble.

It was a massacre, I can accurately state now, looking back. I already had my suspicions at the time, but I had too few points of comparison. They could also execute (I choose the word carefully) the "Barcarolle"—*"Belle nuit, ô nuit d'amour"*—another duo for sopranos, from Offenbach's *Tales of Hoffmann*.

Guy's father, Frédéric, phlegmatically attended these performances, sipping his cognac a little ways away. He wasn't unlikable. He was a thin, very tall man, so tall in fact that he soon became stooped. His son was unlike him in every way, and I wouldn't have put so much as a kopeck on the results of a DNA test. Wherever he was he always appeared to be just visiting, perhaps even and particularly in his own home. All his life he had a mistress whom he housed and fed, and there was so little secrecy surrounding her that I think I always knew her name: Hélène. At the end of these boring Sunday lunches he would often get up from the table, take a cigar, and simply say, "Right." On this decisive pronouncement, he would walk out with a very sketchy goodbye, taking his leave with a wave of his hand. Conversation would pick up again, reignited by Godmother Mone, the high priestess of salvaging appearances.

Frédéric had a brother whose actual name had definitively disappeared behind the more distinctive "Tonton," a nickname for uncle, but I seem to think it was Stéphane. Stéphane had never married and had always lived with his brother. Short, slight, almost thin, he was like Stan Laurel. He was also a private man and no one ever knew him to be in a relationship with a woman. Hearsay therefore lent him another, more secretive life, with men, but nothing ever corroborated this hypothesis. As much an engineer as an inventor, he had made an incredible electric train for my stepfather, a large-scale train with coach roofs that opened to reveal the seats and small figures inside. The locomotive was an exact reproduction on a I/20 scale of the Pacific 230 G from the 1920s. The miniature cast-iron rails were deftly nailed onto oak sleepers. I would have liked this wonder to be exhibited at my parents' house, but my mother preferred her glass-fronted cabinets to display Dresden china marquises, bronze horses, and ivory Buddhas.

When I turned twenty, Tonton handed me the keys to his beige 1955 Peugeot 403, which he was resigned to no longer driving at his age. Her engine and bodywork were in dazzling good shape and I drove all across Italy without a single hitch or power steering. I would have liked to keep that car, but my mother point-blank refused to have this "relic" in the outhouse at the house in the country. She even knocked the building down shortly afterward. I had to resign myself to selling the car.

Frédéric and Stéphane codirected a fountain pen business. I didn't know its name. They manufactured mediocre fountain pens for other companies. Guy's father dealt with financial and marketing matters, his brother with engineering and research.

As a child, I watched the business decline. First there was the crisis of September 1965, when eleven million schoolchildren returned for the new academic year and had permission to write with ballpoints for the first time. Baron Marcel Bich and his revolutionary Bic Cristal caused carnage: the brand's logo became a little orange schoolboy with a large ball-like head and a pen behind him.

"Bic killed me," the headline in *Libération* might have read.

But the fall of the house of Le Tellier was in fact a painful, drawn-out affair. Each generation of their pens met with fiercer competition than its predecessor. The diagnosis for their collapse is simple: first, expensive production in too-small volumes, in the Paris workshops on the rue de la Folie-Méricourt. Then, they dropped further and further behind their competitors' technical developments, due to strategic errors—I remember sarcastic remarks about how stupid cartridges were, when pump-fill pens were so practical. Their design was bland, if not nonexistent, a surprising failing even for that period. Lastly, their commercial position as middle-of-the-range with aspirations was untenable—ah, the peculiar pride in putting a gold nib on a brown Bakelite tube. Schaeffer, Pelikan, Parker, and Waterman—all of whom survived—occupied the inaccessible top-of-the-range.

There is no trace now of their business: type my family name into a search engine along with "fountain" and "pen" and you won't find a single site that refers to them.

The mansion in Chaville had been sold long hence, as had the land and forests. Guy piously kept the press clippings and certificates of sale, proof of past wealth that mostly proved the crass incompetence of a long line of idlers. The Paris home did not belong to them, and very soon the Le Telliers could no longer pay the rent on their apartment. Some of their "very old" pieces of furniture ended their days in my mother's country house, and the two brothers—one now a widower and the other still single—were accepted at a modest retirement home whose fees their owner-craftsmen pensions barely covered. They lived there frugally in three-piece suits originally made to measure but growing more worn by the day.

Their downfall and eventual ruin felt like poetic justice to my working-class mother.

"Ha, now they don't look so clever," I once heard her tell my stepfather, who found nothing to say in reply, because their humiliation was so intimately linked with his own.

· TEN ·

THE NAKED TRUTH

Started this diary today:
eager as I am to note my very
first impressions.
Unpleasant.

RAYMOND QUENEAU, *DORMI PLEURÉ*

I was ten months old when my mother left for England. I have no memory of it at all, and every time I asked my mother about her time in Britain, her only reply would be, "It was only for a year, less even."

And she hastily added, "I came to see you every weekend."

The concept of my mother globetrotting kept me happy for quite a while. But I was a logical child and this struck me as a complicated question. When one day I asked my mother, "Every weekend?" in sudden astonishment, the defense was embellished with a more persuasive "Or you grandmother brought you over."

"By ferry? But it takes far too long. Just getting there—"

"By plane," my mother interjected.

I secured no further information. By plane, then.

This was the late 1950s. Roissy Airport didn't exist; the channel tunnel was a harebrained engineers' dream; budget airlines were yet to be invented. You had to take the plane in Le Bourget and it landed at Gatwick. The cost was exorbitant and a weekly trip would have gobbled up a teacher's pay.

Of course, for the stalwart, there was another flight option, a cheaper and terribly exotic one. You took off from the small airport at Le Touquet in the Pas-de-Calais, and crossed the channel at low altitude to land in Dover fifteen minutes later. This shuttle service was provided by a company called Channel Air Bridge on a funny little propeller freighter, the Bristol 170 Wayfarer. This flying machine was as ugly as it was slow and as noisy as it was sturdy. It had a big round nose which cleaved in two to take in a few vehicles while about twenty passengers traveled in the uncomfortable rear cabin. Its landing gear was fixed; what was the point of retractable landing gear for such a short trip? It would hardly be folded away before it had to come out again. It was an ungainly, very rustic-looking plane, a sort of aluminum whale with wings and a parrot's beak. A slightly merciless pilot once described it as "forty thousand rivets flying in tight formation." The Royal Air Force had commissioned it in the early 1940s to meet the needs of the landings offensive. But the prototype didn't manage to make its maiden flight until December 2, 1945, and the newly established state of peace meant it had to find civil applications: this aerial bridge between England and the Continent was one of them.

That being said, and however adventurous the Le Touquet option might have been, the journey was still an expedition in 1960. The AI Paris–Lille freeway was only at the planning stage, the Nationale I highway was saturated with trucks, and even when you reached Dover, the drive to London was a good two hours more. Which is why my mother's weekly trips still struck me as a spatiotemporal miracle, an exploit worthy of *Star Trek*'s good Mr. Spock and his teleportations.

I subjected my grandmother to an intensive interrogation, and, weary of defending the woefully improbable, she eventually replied, "Your mother came home for school vacations."

These early years of my life are covered with a dense layer of mist made up of so many lies it is impossible to disperse. One thing is certain: very soon after my father left, my mother met the man who would become my stepfather. She supplied far too many versions of how they met for any one of them to be credible. The fact is he joined her in England. In France he had been a school monitor, and then a primary school teacher. He was instantly promoted at the Wallington School for Boys, and he became a teaching assistant, then a teacher. They were married in

England in October 1959, as soon as my mother's divorce came through.

For a long time I believed that the British episode lasted only a few months, a year at the very most, but when my stepfather died and I was sorting through paperwork, I discovered that he and my mother did not return to France until March 1961, when I was nearly four. My mother did not witness my first steps or hear my first word, and it was my grandfather who told her I'd learned to read. Throughout this period I stayed with my parents only very intermittently. Because they were working, I often spent my days in kindergarten, a sort of intensive language course where I learned at my cost that for "pipi" you said "wee-wee." Almost my only memory of my early childhood in England is of humiliation heightened by a strong smell of urine. For good measure, we can add to that the black swans—rather ill-tempered creatures—on an artificial pond, and the too-sweet smell of poor-quality cacao from the nearby Rowntree's chocolate factory.

When I turned five, my trips lasted longer. Guy and my mother continued teaching in Croydon for three or four months a year, but I now went with them. I attended the same primary school on each occasion, Wallington School for Boys. At the time, classes in Britain were ruled over by evil little tyrants, propelled to the rank of overseers of order and discipline: school prefects. Hard to tell whether their position was the root of their sadism or, conversely, whether they were selected on the grounds of this predisposition. The one who "oversaw" my class over a three-year period was called Andrew Peacock, with all the posturing that name implies. I immediately became his whipping boy, and he chose me for punishments of all sorts. In his defense, being French, friendless, two years younger than he was, and destined not to stay at the school, I was the perfect target. And so—with the complicit indifference of the teaching staff, who felt that maintaining the peace required a scapegoat to be found—I was the French frog, a "thicko," "retarded"; and this last was because I was slow to retaliate, because my mastery of English was initially poor. The fascinating English education system of that era fills me with a profound aversion to this day, and no, I don't really like the atmosphere at Hogwarts in *Harry Potter*.

I returned to Paris for good at the age of seven.

We moved into a small apartment on rue Duhesme. Really small: beds, table, chairs—they all folded away. When I walked past the building a few years ago I saw a "For Sale" sign hanging on the balcony. I went to have a look: successive owners had transformed it, but hadn't succeeded in making it larger. It measured—with thanks to the Carrez law on real estate floor area—three hundred square feet. We won't mention the price, too obscene.

It was at about this time that my mother entered into a battle that lasted for years: I was to change my name. She had always loathed the name Goupil, which is another word for "fox" with all the possible undesirable connotations; and while she was married to my begetter, she had even asked him to change his name. She now felt it indispensable that I had a different one; she opted first for her father's family name, Michel, but her efforts were doomed to fail. She then enrolled me for the next year at primary school under the name Le Tellier, and convinced the school's administrative system not only that I would refuse to respond to any other, but also that calling the disturbed child I was by the name Goupil could trigger a breakdown of sorts.

Then she started legal proceedings. She drafted dozens of letters to the district attorney for me, and I had to copy them all out. I came across one of her drafts in which I explained that my begetter had "abandoned me shortly after I was born," that I wanted to have my stepfather's name, and incidentally I called him "Daddy," because he had "taken me in" shortly afterward and had even "adopted" me. I signed it "Hervé Le Tellier, age 9, sixth-grade pupil."

It was at about the same age that I learned, during the course of an adult conversation, that my mother had had an abortion in Switzerland a few years earlier. The moment they realized the child playing with his Lego set had turned to listen, there was silence. My grandmother took me aside and explained that it had been an "accident," and my mother hadn't wanted any more children at the time. But my mother wanted to say more on the subject and gave me full explanations several times: She'd done it "for me." Guy would naturally have been more attached to "his" child and he would have forsaken me, even turned against me. Thanks to her, I therefore knew I had been responsible for the death of a little brother or sister, and also that I couldn't trust my daddy.

But I soon realized that it was difficult to give credence to anything my mother said. It wasn't that she particularly liked lying, but accepting the truth was just asking too much of her. So she accumulated lies and imposed them on everyone else.

Grandpa had fallen out with his younger brother, Émile, a long time earlier, although I never knew why. They didn't see each other, or talk to each other. At sixty, the depressive, melancholy Émile hanged himself. My mother was first to hear the news and decided to hide this tragedy from her father. Like everyone else in the family, I was given orders not to mention it under any circumstances: "Your grandfather is very sick, you mustn't talk to him about it." Even so, on several occasions I tried to find out why Émile had committed suicide. I secured no answer other than a shrug of her shoulders. There was madness in the family and the best thing to do was make it disappear—even if under a cloak of silence.

When Grandpa died, his father, Joseph was ninety-five; he still lived in his garret room on the boulevard Ornano.

My mother decided to hide his elder son's death from the old man, just as she had managed to camouflage the younger son's: Grandpa was traveling in the Middle East, Émile had moved to Biarritz. When, full of suspicion, Joseph tried to find out more, my mother ardently embellished her lies. She left him in ignorance right up until his death, three years later.

But most revealing of all was the Otto incident. Otto was my German pen pal, who was twelve, like me. It wasn't a friendship so much as something engineered by adults, the linguistic friendship equivalent of a forced marriage, which can lead to enduring unjustified loathing toward an entire race. All of us—my aunt, uncle, cousins, and parents—were in the mountains and we were waiting for Otto to arrive. His older sister, Sandra, proud to have recently passed her driving test, was bringing him in her spanking new Beetle.

There was a telephone call, sudden agitation; my uncle Serge and my stepfather immediately left. I was playing Monopoly with my cousins when my mother came to see us: Sandra had just called her and it was a real shame but Otto was sick, terrible pneumonia, and he couldn't come for the week.

"Listen," my mother added, looking at me intently, "it's not that bad, you'll see him in the summer vacation."

I was very disappointed. I was not particularly bothered that Otto wouldn't be coming, but I wouldn't see Sandra, who had been a powerful erotic fantasy of mine since I'd seen her swimming in the pool of their luxury villa in Bavaria one evening, and had glimpsed her beautiful naked breasts.

The game continued and I finally managed to buy up the glamorously expensive rue de la Paix. My mother and aunt had slunk off to a bedroom alone and were arguing. We snuck up to the door.

"We mustn't tell them," my mother said quietly. "It'll ruin their vacation."

"But honestly, we can't hide this from them," my aunt retorted, sobbing. "Can you imagine? How horrific."

"If you decide to tell them the truth, Raphy, we're going back to Paris right away," said my mother.

My uncle and stepfather arrived home just then. My uncle looked serious: he sat my cousins and me down and told us that, as Sandra and Otto were crossing the German border, they'd had a car crash, on the freeway. Sandra was seriously injured and Otto was dead.

My uncle went further, saying Sandra was in a coma and her little brother had died instantly, he hadn't suffered, and was actually asleep when the accident happened. A ceremony would be arranged for all of us in the chapel early the next morning. We would pray for Otto and particularly for Sandra. Then, because there was nothing we could do, we three children went off for our ski lesson.

My mother was at the far end of the room, devastated, crushed. I was distraught but her gaze was so unfocused I couldn't catch her eye. I think I remember her coming to hug me, but she never mentioned Otto's invented pneumonia again. I'd seen her lie to me for the first time, and I knew it would now be impossible to trust her.

All the lies she'd already served up came back to me and there were hundreds still to come. My stepfather didn't have any sort of aristocratic title, but I heard my mother claiming he was a count, insisting that he confirm the fact, which he did awkwardly. His years as a primary school teacher, which she deemed to be beneath her, were erased and I saw him promoted straight to the rank of a high school English teacher. My mother, who'd attended a few seminars at a University Institute of Technology, instantly became a university professor. She joined the ranks of those with the prestigious *"aggrégation"* teaching qualification via some obscure internal promotion, and managed to convince herself that she really had achieved this qualification.

Everything was aimed to dress up annoying truths. I had to uphold her fictions, especially as she frequently made me an accomplice to them. At sixteen I dropped my first year of advanced math and only months later failed my first year of university. But as far as all the family were concerned I obtained my degree; I didn't dare contradict my mother when she forced on me math diplomas that I only actually achieved the following year. When I left home at eighteen, my mother hid the fact from my grandmother, even though she lived only two floors down. If and when I dropped by, my mother always muttered, "Whatever you do, don't tell your grandmother you've left home, she'd die of a broken heart."

But my grandmother knew, she had from the start, and she survived.

ELEVEN

CUVILLY

Our ancestors liked the countryside: they
Strolled through it and didn't look at it.

JULES RENARD, *JOURNAL*

Thanks to her father, my mother had a house in the country.

That description is misleading. First of all, it wasn't really in the country but in one of those little Picardy villages with lines of small farms along a main road. The place wasn't completely deserted: granted, the school had closed, but it still had a grocery store, a bakery, a café that sold newspapers and had a French billiards table, and of course a church. It had the words "Oh my, the Good Lord is good!" on the pediment. This was not meant humorously, particularly as, come to think of it, "Oh my, the Virgin Mary's a virgin!" would have been funnier.

As for the house itself, it would be more honest to describe it as a farm, only half a farm even: it had been divided into two lots and the farmyard had been cut into two smaller yards by an imposing stone wall, although it was not high enough to stop me expediting all my soccer balls into the neighbor's yard when I played there as a child.

The term "main road," on the other hand, was too modest a term: it was in fact the Nationale 1 highway between Paris and Lille. The A1 freeway had admittedly diverted some of the traffic, which was very heavy right up to the seventies, but every minute—or nearly—a semitrailer thundered through just yards from the dining room, rattling the windowpanes. With the passing years, I could gauge the progress of soundproofing techniques, but the brick walls still shook just as much when thirty-tonners went past.

The village was called Cuvilly, and my grandfather, who initially owned the house, had rather pleasingly baptized its inhabitants Cuviles, spitefully stressing the "viles"—which was pure calumny because they were in fact Cuvillois. He had bought the house in the thirties and, having accommodated his parents there for a while, made it his own second home after the war, despite the region having the poorest amount of sunshine in all of France, and rainfall very favorable to weeping willows. It was here that, as an autocratic paterfamilias, he gathered together his daughters, sons-in-law, and grandchildren during the summer vacation and the Christmas holidays. Even so, I have very few memories apart from a nativity scene made of brown paper, and brightly colored tinsel on a Christmas tree. When my mother became senile, she took to saying repeatedly, "We were so happy there," but I have so little idea of what shared happiness she means that I imagine she is referring to her teenage years and the time before I was born.

Every time my stepfather walked past the huge Nordmann pine planted at the far end of the yard, he would say, "That's incredible, to think that was the little Christmas tree from 1967…"

One day, weary of this endless repetition, I decided to avoid the trite pronouncement by preempting it with a "Hey! Isn't that the little Christmas tree from 1967?"

All the same, Guy replied earnestly, "Yes, it is. It's incredible, when you think of it."

My grandfather died during the "May 1968 events." He was buried in the family vault in the village cemetery. That could have been the end of Cuvilly if, when the legacy was announced by the notary, my mother hadn't bought out her sister, who sold her share with no hesitation or regrets. Even though my mother would never lay chrysanthemums on her father's grave, she couldn't countenance moving away from his bones or abandoning this house full of memories of the happy times she'd spent with him. Perhaps she was also hoping to perpetuate the family get-togethers. But her sister, who was no fool, preferred sunshine in summer and snow in winter.

All the same, from then on my mother never stopped extending and improving the thankless building—not that any of these alterations led anyone to spend so much as a weekend there. Because my mother and her husband visited Cuvilly no more frequently than before, except to oversee the progress of mammoth projects. A small fortune was sunk into the place: dormer windows popped up in the tiled roof, halogen spotlights dutifully lit up the trees at night, then centrally controlled electric shutters were fitted, and a solid oak staircase replaced a metal ladder up to the converted loft space...the real estate version of aggressive therapy on a patient who wants to be left to die.

The house originally had four bedrooms but ended up with a total of seven, which might seem a lot for a couple with one child and not a single friend. My mother had given every bedroom its own bathroom, each one fitted with a hip bath, a washing facility that is now long forgotten (and with good reason), the love child of a monstrous union between an uncomfortable throne and a chamber pot. You couldn't shower properly in the thing, and you couldn't bathe in it at all, but at least the colors of the enamel were retro: ochre, mauve, aqua, violet...And as a sign of the times, each bathroom also had a bidet, an intimate hygiene device that became exotic because it was so utterly condemned as uncool, despite its existence being acknowledged as far back as 1739 by the dictionary *Trésor de la langue française* (Treasures of the French Language). Its progressive disappearance, which some may regret, could be evidence of a backward step in intimate hygiene, of more widespread use of showers, or of decisive advances in the quality of toilet paper. But there would be too much to say for the question to be explored further here.

At the dawn of the new millennium, my parents told me they had something for me: a gift, as is permitted by law, to the sum of thirty thousand euros, free of tax. I thanked them because I was paying off a crippling mortgage at the time, but they proudly informed me that the sum had actually been spent buying up the adjoining field, which was now in my name. They had even instantly knocked down the wall that separated it from their yard, thereby annexing this land of mine and amply planting it with trees.

When I told a friend about this "field business" he put things in perspective.

"What are you complaining about?" he asked. "Do you know what my parents gave me for my fortieth birthday? A concession in perpetuity in the cemetery, right next to them."

"Cuvilly" was decorated in the very assertive bad taste of the seventies, triumphantly featuring Vasarelyesque op-art wallpaper, exposed beams, and rustic internal plastering. The house had become a sort of attic store, accumulating furniture my mother had variously inherited and that she liked to think was "of value" because it was, as she kept reiterating, "very old." The Henri II Brittany table and its carved chairs in gloomy dark wood lived alongside Louis XV wingback chairs upholstered in pink silk and inlaid Empire dressers. Added to these were soft furnishing horrors, deep velvet sofas with busy, garish patterns, and improbable poufs in fluorescent plastic, filled with creaking polystyrene beads, things that swallowed up your body and from which you could only extricate yourself with ridiculous contortions that were downright painful for the more advanced in years. Not to mention all the pieces that had gone out of fashion because they were dated almost as soon as they were bought. On the walls, various daubings vied for attention: bouquets of roses, brightly colored Deauville-school oils, and assorted watercolors of the heathland in flower in the spring.

When, years later, shortly after my stepfather died, I took on the task of selling the house and therefore emptying it first, I found that the few things I'd kept there had been stolen by the scurrilous key-holders. I also learned that the items of furniture I'd stored there after a house move had been given away to the cleaner by my mother, because the woman liked them. They were "cluttering up the place." She hadn't seen any need to discuss this with me.

"Listen," she said, swooping her eyes to the heavens, "they were just old relics."

She meant this sincerely: she had already adhered to this very personal logic in the seventies, when she used a secondhand-goods dealer—who was only too happy to help her—to get rid of a 1911 Delahaye 44 with a V6 engine, which had been slumbering in the barn.

I may flatter myself that my own possessions found takers, but not one antiques dealer took an interest in that unsigned furniture, the bric-a-brac dealers played hard to get, and in the end the house clearance people I called in sighed with disappointment. That's how these "very old" and "highly valuable" pieces of furniture ended their careers at a secondhand depot where they went conspicuously unnoticed by regular customers. The building itself was on the market for years without attracting any takers. Buyers wanting to live by the side of a major road in an oversized house that sometimes had to be heated in June were a rare breed. It eventually found a buyer only at a derisory price, although it was less insulting than some of the offers had been. With this I calculated that for twenty-five years my parents had estimated the house was worth nearly three times its true value, and this had tipped them into the flattering side with the three hundred thousand taxpayers liable for wealth tax.

But that's the price you pay for maternal pride.

TWELVE

THE SWISS ACCOUNT

No money, no Switzerland.

JEAN RACINE, *LES PLAIDEURS*

O n April 18, 1906, the San Andreas Fault decided to wake up: an earthquake measuring 7.8 tore through San Francisco Bay at 5:00 a.m. local time, and then, when Wall Street opened an hour later, it ransacked insurance company share prices the world over. Threatened with ruin by the hundreds of millions of dollars in damages, they naturally turned to their reinsurers, those insurers' insurers, including Winterthur, the Swiss equivalent of Britain's Lloyd's. The share price of Winterthur in Zurich first came apart, then collapsed completely over three days, in time with the implacable advances of fires ravaging San Francisco, which nothing managed to extinguish. Faced with the prospect of defaulting on its employees' wages, the company offered to remunerate some of them with shares that had no face value at the time.

Among them was a very young man who made the bold and visionary decision to accept the arrangement: when in 1907, Winterthur was pronounced not to be responsible for this natural catastrophe, its share price bounced back even higher than it had been before. The man was rich, and a rich Swiss is doubly so. The depression of the 1930s barely affected his fortune, perhaps even accrued it, and he married a pretty Frenchwoman, Suzanne, fifteen years his junior, well before World War II broke out.

In the early 1980s, my stepfather grew close to a distant cousin of his. It was Suzanne, now the insurer's widow. Suzanne was childless and a ripe old age. It turned out she was still rich and had the use of the bank account—the "secret" bank account, if we can forgive that Swiss pleonasm—born of the California earthquake. Too tired to make the return trips from Switzerland, she left the traveling to Guy, who started making very fruitful journeys.

His cousin named him as her only inheritor before she died, aged nearly one hundred, in 1990. My stepfather was suddenly a big step ahead. Which was unexpected. As a distant cousin, he paid substantial inheritance tax, which would have been still more substantial if (and this was surely just an oversight) he hadn't neglected to tell the French tax authorities about his new Swiss bank account.

When Guy died, I went to see the bank manager in Lausanne with my mother, who was in mourning and slightly disoriented. I had no idea what the sum was, as my stepfather had been highly secretive. What I found, let's cut to the chase, was a tidy haul, the value of a handsome Paris apartment. I then had access to the account history, although only for the last three years, and I was amazed by what I saw: Guy had withdrawn large sums from the account, always in cash.

The method he used to bring the money into France was well known to the tax authorities. No bills actually crossed the frontier. It was "compensation," a perfectly legal money laundering system: a French fraudster—at best a butcher, if not a pimp or a trafficker—handed over cash to a representative of the Swiss bank in France, and he then passed the parcel to a French citizen short of cash and keen on invisibility. The sum was debited from the recipient's account and transferred to the fraudster's account, with the bank taking 5 percent of the figure on each transaction, in other words 10 percent. Laundering pays.

I tried to convince my mother to declare this account, which was now shared. I was in an awkward situation: at the time I wrote a humorous column for the morning and electronic editions of *Le Monde* and, when appropriate to the news, I railed against fiscal fraud. Hollande had just been elected; there was an atmosphere of openness: any revelation about this bank account, however hypothetical, would have put a major national daily in a tricky position. I arranged to see Érik Izraelewicz, who had just been made

CEO and would die of a heart attack on the premises a year later. Izra saw me briefly but I didn't have much to say.

"I've just inherited a Swiss bank account, a non-declared account. I'll make sure it's all regularized."

"Oh? Okay. I thought you were coming to talk about a raise. Do you have a tax lawyer?"

"I've found one, the only one who didn't ask to be paid only in cash."

"Good luck then. This'll make you laugh, you're the third person in three months to tell me the same story."

I started the regularization process with the French tax authorities. It was then and only then that the Swiss bank consented to release to them—and simultaneously to me—information about earlier years. Guy had left no accounting documents, even in the safety-deposit box held at the bank.

I've already mentioned that I was amazed by my stepfather's cash withdrawals. To be honest, I was dumbstruck: in the early 1980s, the funds in the account were worth over forty million francs; that's more than six million euros. Now, despite respectable interest payments, it was almost empty: Guy had withdrawn something in the region of 250,000 euros every year. Had he lived another two years, he would have totally drained Suzanne's legacy—after the fines and costs of regularization of course, but I'll leave the sums to readers who are tax experts. Please forgive this accumulation of figures, but if you add their pensions and private incomes, my parents had spent over three hundred thousand euros a year. My mother, who was already bewildered, said she knew nothing, was "flabbergasted."

It's worth pointing out, for posterity, that in 2011 that sum represented the price of a one-bedroom apartment in Paris, a small manor house in the Périgord (in need of renovation), twenty years at minimum wage, twice the annual income of a surgeon, or ten days' salary for an Apple director—seen another way: a Margherita pizza with extra arugula every day for a century. It was a lot.

Hats off to him: the bottom line is that at that price, the Dismally Dull Guy was raised to the ranks of a fictional character.

Sadly, the men at the tax office aren't too keen on novels.

"What is there to prove," asked the tax inspector to whom I admitted the unexplained disappearance of funds, "that your stepfather didn't hand the money over to you in cash and you've hidden it?"

His question, which was perfectly fair, caught me off guard.

"You do understand," he went on, "it's the first thought anyone would have, quite legitimately. And it's very common, between parents and children."

That last sentence was a revelation: the concept that Guy might have bequeathed me his legacy, secretly or not, had never occurred to me. I had to convince the tax inspector that I never thought I'd see the color of this money, and prove I'd had to organize my life so that I was never financially dependent on my stepfather.

I had a few documents to support this: years earlier, when I couldn't pull together all the money I needed to buy an apartment, I'd had to reconcile myself to asking Guy for help. He'd agreed to lend me the sum, but made me duly sign an acknowledgment of debt, "for the tax office." It took me four years to reimburse that money, which corresponded with what he was spending every month. At around the same time, Guy gave a studio apartment to my son, who was twelve at the time, to reduce his taxes. But he had kept for himself the usufruct of it, and therefore the rent, so that—it was perfectly clear—I wouldn't pick up on it. I had deduced that this fortune, if it existed at all, would skip a generation at best. While I laid out these facts to the tax inspector, I thought I could see a glimmer of compassion in his eyes.

At the end of the day, the tax authority restricted itself to taking 60 percent, interest and taxes included. The nouveau riche inheritor that I had become kept the rest, while the spread-the-love Trotskyite in me pretended, rather shamefacedly, to sleep. Still, this part of me did take pride in signing a check that would fund a primary schoolteacher for a whole career. "When your bank balance looks good, things can get bad," was the philosophical summary of the man in Lausanne who had become my banker.

But how had Guy spent this money? Gambling, drugs, blackmail, a double life, an exorbitant but invisible lifestyle? There were a limited number of hypotheses. I explored them all.

Guy did not gamble. Surrendering his assets to the vagaries of chance would have been unbearable to him. He had never set foot in a casino, never hung around racecourses, or even bought a single lottery ticket at the corner shop. Still, they say you can easily blow a hundred thousand euros on the apparently harmless Tac-O-Tac lottery. No, Guy had a cautious, fearful nature: he had chosen responsible options for the management of the Swiss account, preferring a low return to alternatives that involved any risk. I remember him rolling his eyes and shrugging his shoulders when Apple shares dropped to an irrational twenty dollars or so in 2001, and I advised him to invest in them if he had any funds.

The thought of Guy on drugs makes me smile. He hadn't smoked for a long time, on his wife's orders because it made her cough. If he agreed to drink, it was a glass of port before dinner, perhaps a pastis. He didn't drink wine, or if he did, very little. One Sunday at lunchtime I caught him slipping sweetener and water into his glass of *Haut-Médoc*—a bottle I had brought. And if he'd been a cocaine addict, a whole medical thesis could have been based on him: "a unique example of a lymphatic reaction to a tropane alkaloid: the Guy Le Tellier case."

I had trouble imagining what grounds there could have been for blackmail. A shameful sexual practice filmed by some reprobate, a murder to which there was a witness, a hidden child who threatened to go public? It was all delightful, but not very plausible.

The double life was the best option. But a double life means you actually have a life in the first place, and Guy seemed to spend the best part of his time not having one. He rarely left the marital home, except to go to the drugstore, where his consumption of medication must have elicited if not admiration, at least enthusiasm. He could be reached on his cell phone at any time, or almost, and my mother was never far from him. May his spirit forgive me if I'm underestimating him.

"Professional women?" the Swiss banker had suggested (he was a great exponent of discreet terminology).

"Whores?" I asked more prosaically, in order both to check I'd understood properly and to make things a little awkward.

"Yes."

"Are they that expensive?"

"I don't know," he said cautiously. "I imagine it depends."

And why not, after all? With the uninhibited candor that goes hand in hand with senility, my mother had made a point of telling me she'd banned him from her bed more than twenty years earlier. She had discovered—although, as was usual with her, there was nothing to prove it—that he "hung around with" prostitutes. Just because once when they were walking along avenue Foch he had pointed to a parked pickup with a piece of red cloth tied to the handle of the rear door, a discreet sign—according to him—of a vehicle adapted for the sex industry.

"You see, he knew, that's proof enough that he used them," she said, in no doubt at all.

But almost immediately, and unafraid of contradicting herself, she'd told me that shortly after her husband had had a triple bypass and a pacemaker fitted, the cardiologist had whispered to her, "My dear, a word of advice: not too often, and not too wild."

Guy was therefore not the perfect candidate for the unbridled life of a libertine, even with remunerated partners. And had he paid the eye-watering prices for rare or complicated requirements—but here, it goes without saying, I'm talking way beyond my personal experience—it still would not have cost the equivalent of a Porsche every three months.

And so for the final hypothesis: a hidden lifestyle. A handsome oxymoron, that. Hiding wealth we can imagine, but how to disguise expenditure? Eating caviar in secret? And if there had been a lust for spending, what traces of it were there?

"We spent without counting the cost," my mother did admit to me proudly when, in my attempts to understand,

I asked her. But nothing in their home had any true value. The hundreds of pairs of size-nine flats could overflow from closets, my mother's six mink coats could be made to measure, and a facelift every five years can't be cheap, but the sums were still nowhere near adding up. They paid no rent, they drove a French sedan that they rarely replaced, and, although they sank idiotic amounts of money into that wretched "country house," they had no real financial burdens.

I got to the point where I imagined that this money repatriated over the years was still somewhere in France. In some place he alone knew and he had, as they say, taken that knowledge to the grave.

In his stiff handwriting on an index card, Guy had made a note of all necessary information in the event of his death. There was the phone number of the Swiss banker, the reference numbers for various accounts, savings accounts and life insurance, and even the code for his safety-deposit box. But in the top right-hand corner on the back of the card were four mysterious letters, written in bold capitals, underlined with a squiggly line: HAST.

It didn't mean anything to me. My mother knew nothing about it, or had forgotten. My son had never heard the word.

I searched, of course. A *hast* in French is a kind of weapon, a javelin, or a spit for roasting meat, and the word is worth seven points in Scrabble. It's also a brand of men's shirts, but not the make my stepfather wore. A fashion start-up. It could stand for Hawaii-Aleutian Standard Time, or the Higher Ability Selection Test of British secondary schools. The Hammond Academy of Science and Technology. The archaic, and very Shakespearean, English declension of "you have: thou hast."

It's German too: *Du hast nie verstanden.* You never understood.

Indeed.

· THIRTEEN ·

FRAGMENTS OF CHILDHOOD

With children, a good slap
never did any harm.

IAN MONK, "AVANT DE NAÎTRE" *PLOUK TOWN*

I have so few childhood memories that in writing this
book I had to delve deep to come up with only a handful. By the simple fact that they've survived they're
bound to be extraordinary.

The bedroom where I sleep on rue Duhesme is half
a room because a gray muslin curtain cuts it off from
the half that acts as a living room and where, in spite of
everything, an upright piano and two small armchairs
have been accommodated. My bed is a red fold-up with a
metal mesh frame, and I'm not aware that it's particularly
narrow. There's also a dresser, a small desk, and a pale
blue velvet horse on springs that I climb onto and jig-
gle in every direction, holding on to a sort of handlebar.
Sometimes I wake early in the morning and join Guy and
my mother; they sleep in their strange closet-bed that

lifts up during the day, given that the room is also the living room.

I'm in the little extra space that serves as a hallway. The carpeting is black and close-cropped. I'm playing marbles: I line them up in battle order; the green ones are the allies, the rust ones the enemy coalition, the big ones are commanding officers. Like millions of other children at this exact moment, I can hear the title music of *Bonne nuit les petits* (Goodnight, Little Ones) from the small black-and-white TV; it's played on a reed pipe and I couldn't care less that it's by Pergolesi. But I don't want to go to bed, I make some of my troops start an encirclement, I'm Leonidas at Thermopylae, Napoleon at Austerlitz. I can play like this for hours, without tiring of it.

I go with my parents to do the shopping, strolling along aisles. When we come to the checkout, my mother hands over coupons for discounts on some product or other. The cashier looks at them, hands them back, and tells her that, sadly, the expiration date on the coupons has passed. My mother rebels; the young woman explains again, patiently, that the offer is no longer valid. My mother raises her voice and suddenly, with no warning, she blanches with rage and starts screaming at the cashier that the girl's just a "pathetic idiot" who "failed all her exams," and she—my mother—doesn't have to "take orders" from her; she insists on seeing the manager. Terrified, I take a step back. "It's not all that important…" Guy ventures.

"Oh, coming from you, naturally, from you, of course..."
my mother snaps, demented with anger, almost spitting.
Frozen in terror, I watch her as she hurls the contents of
the cart on the ground, the shrill orange of broken eggs
spreads, she shrieks that she'll "never come back to this
store full of morons," and as she steps out the door she
lobs a final "fucking bitch." My stepfather runs after her,
I turn around, the cashier has tears in her eyes, everyone
is looking at us, I'm ashamed. We're leaving, I don't say a
word; Guy walks, hangdog, one step behind my mother,
while she kicks out at car tires, muttering incomprehensibly. I understand now just how much my mother frightens
me, and Guy almost as much. I'm no longer safe, I'm at
her mercy.

The Citroën Ami 8 is trundling through the darkness,
we're coming home from the country and I'm lying on the
rear seat, dozing. The red lights at the porte de Clignan-
court interrupt the rhythm and I wake, the asthmatic sound
of the twin cylinders smothers my parents' conversation, and
I open my very nearsighted eyes to the hazy lights of Paris.

I'm eleven, I'm in the country, it's the fall, sparks dance
behind the opaque glass on the big oil-fired stove. A sudden thought bowls me over: because I can remember facts
from before this day itself, which means I have a past, I
obviously exist. A sort of "I remember therefore I am."
I decree that my conscious life begins at that moment.
I've forgotten—and it's quite an omission—what specific

memory initiated this; perhaps recalling my grandfather's death a few months earlier.

I read. A lot. The Famous Five, Bob Morane, then Jules Verne, Alexandre Dumas, and H. G. Wells. Also the ten-volume *Grand Larousse* encyclopedia bound in green leather; I open the volumes at random and devour the entry on Genghis Khan just as readily as the one devoted to hydrazotoluene. Until the age of thirteen I had no trouble avoiding boredom at home. I read while I ate my lunch all alone; I ran back to my books as soon as dinner was finished; I read at night, under the covers, with a flashlight. I also read at the bookshop.

The bookshop lady. I never really knew her name (Suzanne? Éliane?) and definitely not her family name, but I would never be able to count up all the hours I spent in her shop. It was just downstairs from our apartment on rue Ordener, and tiny, no more than a hundred square feet, and it was a stationer's too. Sometimes there would be as many as three children sitting on the floor reading, occasionally playing. Among them were Jehanne and her brother, Renaud. They lived in my building, on the second floor, their parents never stopped arguing, and the bookshop was a refuge for them too. One evening we had to leave and I stole a book; it was Pierre Boulle's *The Planet of the Apes*. Back home, I put it on my bed but found I couldn't bring myself even to open it, I was so paralyzed with shame. I'd stolen from the bookseller, I would be driven out of

Paradise. I went downstairs to return it, almost in tears, but she had already lowered the metal shutter. I took it back the next morning, stammering apologies. She smiled at me, consoled me. I was allowed to stay in Paradise.

I was, I admit, drawn to science fiction, particularly from the States. The publishers Marabout and J'ai Lu provided the bulk of my preadolescent education: Clifford D. Simak's *City* gave me a lesson in morality, Daniel Keyes's *Flowers for Algernon* threw me into despair, Philip K. Dick's *The Man in the High Castle* taught me the potentiality of history.

I could with complete sincerity defend the notion that science fiction—that purveyor of universes and paradigms—is a wonderful pathway toward questioning the world, which could be a definition of wisdom.

.
. .

I've never cared much for religion. At Wallington School for Boys in the 1960s the Church of England was closely bound to the state, and in my early years of English I unenthusiastically stammered through the Protestant hymns that began each day, thirty minutes before the start of lessons. There were hundreds of us boys, lined up on benches in our black uniforms in a huge hall, sitting down and standing up and sitting back down and standing up again, along with the teachers, according to a changeable ritual whose tenets and aims I never grasped. None of it convinced me much. And I also struggled with Santa Claus.

My mother's faith was vague. She and her sister had been educated in a Catholic school, and she had accepted this without haggling. It was "important" to her father, and little Marceline was anything but rebellious. But we never went to church, even for Christmas mass; nor was there any suggestion of saying my prayers at bedtime, and because we never talked about anything at home, the question of religion never cropped up in this absence of conversation. All the same, my mother also thought it was "important" for me, even though no supporting argument—except her authority over me—was ever put forward.

That is most likely why, once back in France, she gave me no choice and signed me up for Bible study. The sessions were always at the end of the afternoon, in the school's basement. I quite liked these neon-lit get-togethers where the catechist had told us we really "mustn't think twice about interrupting him at any time" to ask questions, because "these weren't lessons, but an introduction to God and faith." I was soon excluded, precisely because I asked questions. I wanted to know—my mother told me later because I had no memory of this—whether the all-powerful God was all-powerful enough to choose not to exist. There was no malice in my inventing this daft syllogism, a sort of reversal—and no less absurd than the original—of Anselm of Canterbury's ontological argument for the existence of God. So I protested against the injustice that had been done to me, but there was nothing for it: the catechist did not want me back.

Despite this appalling track record, I took my first Holy Communion: draped in a white alb, lost in a long procession of supplicants, I slowly made my way toward the bishop in the Church of the Holy Trinity in Paris. When I finally reached the guy, I knelt piously and clearly uttered the vow I'd learned by heart. Unfortunately, impressed by the setting and the solemnity of the occasion, I inverted the words and enunciated as distinctly as I could, "I turn to Satan and I renounce Christ forever." Then I opened my mouth wide to welcome the host and I was blessed with a halfhearted gesture from a weary priest who hadn't listened very attentively to what I'd said. That was in May 1968. A few days later I went to see the wreckage of the barricades on the rue Gay-Lussac, and the streets with their cobblestones ripped out. Another few days on and my grandfather was dying of leukemia in the hospital. All these memories are vague, but the color of my own personal May '68 is a peculiar mixture of white, red, and black.

Along came 1969. I was twelve. I remember the date and my age so clearly because I was building a scale model of LEM, the Lunar Experimental Module, and it stood on my desk, waiting to be finished. I chose LEM because in July of that year I had stayed up late with my cousins to watch live as men landed on the moon. We were out in the country that night, and the big black-and-white cathode-ray television broadcast fuzzy images. My little cousin had fallen asleep and I'd listened to Jacques Sallebert—the French TV company ORTF's special correspondent in Houston—commenting on the images from Apollo II. In the middle of the night, at 3:56 a.m., Neil Armstrong had transmitted live as he took a small step for himself and a giant leap for mankind. In New York, coming just before 10:00 p.m. and therefore hitting prime time, the event had principally been the magnificent propaganda show it had been intended to be. But for a child in France, the lateness of the hour added to the sense of wonder.

Two months later it was September and I moved into ninth grade. My stepfather had a new colleague, a Monsieur Plachet, who—a real rarity—came to visit. Monsieur Plachet was between forty and sixty years old, a wide range which confirms that I really was twelve, and if I described him with any accuracy today I'd be lying. Most important, Monsieur Plachet was a Jehovah's Witness. I don't know how or why this happened, but my parents gave him permission to meet me, and over the course of several weeks, he took it upon himself to convert me. Neither my mother nor my stepfather had, as far as I know, become members of the sect, which makes those Wednesday sessions all the more outlandish.

Monsieur Plachet met me alone, contrary to tradition. Because, need I remind you of the joke, Jehovah's Witnesses are like testicles: they come in pairs, one is smaller than the other, and however hard they bang on the door, they never get in.

Let's break the suspense: the conversion project failed.

As luck would have it, of all the monotheistic religions spawned by Judaism, the Jehovah's Witnesses' is the craziest, making absolutely no concessions to the real world when most of the others, whether they like it or not and on pain of losing all credibility, have had to accept submitting to reality—even if Moses does still part the Red Sea, Jesus multiplies loaves of bread, and Mohammed travels on a winged horse. So Monsieur Plachet really did believe the world was created, and that this happened over seven days, he believed in the flood and Noah's ark, and most of all he believed that after the final judgment and the Resurrection, 144,000 people chosen by God would run the future world, while the rest of humanity—all safely resuscitated too—would serve them. To this day I wonder what Monsieur Plachet could actually have taught. Natural sciences and history are excluded de facto, as is math, which does have a whole branch called logic. Modern languages, French, and physical education were more compatible with exercising his faith.

It wasn't difficult resisting Monsieur Plachet's fables, but my debates with him were not very theological. With the full weight of my twelve years behind me, I mostly battled against details I found unacceptable: the earth was a few thousand years old, and the dinosaurs had lived with Adam and Eve in Paradise, where all the animals were vegetarians, even the terrifying *Tyrannosaurus rex*, which I'd so frequently had devouring my plastic triceratops. I was disappointed and skeptical...that really was quite a lot of canines for nibbling on carrots.

Between my Wednesday sessions, I read the Bible, particularly Genesis, but also any popular-science magazines I could lay my hands on, far more to fuel our discussions than to trip him up, and as soon as he arrived I would shower him with new questions. Let's say Noah did put the animals on his ark two by two. Including kangaroos, which had come all the way from Australia? Yes, Monsieur Plachet replied, hesitantly. I'd read in the big *Life* encyclopedia that there were tens of thousands of species of beetle. How did they all fit on Mr. Noah's boat? Monsieur Plachet seemed a little peeved by this teeming, crawling invasion. What about the age of the sun? What about the Grand Canyon? And the shape of glacial valleys? Monsieur Plachet had forgotten everything from his school days. In my view, God was just a stopgap for his boundless lack of knowledge, while in his view, the devil alone was the inspiration for all my satanic riddles.

It lasted only a month, and Monsieur Plachet never came back, after one final question about Lake Titicaca, although I forget its exact terms—my mother frequently discussed this with me afterward because he had repeated the question to her, shaking his head in despair.

So it was that, while I was still a child, I was exposed to the harebrained theories of an apocalyptic sect and no one worried about the consequences. In my teens, I wanted to know how these sessions had come about. My stepfather shrugged, as he always did, meaning that yet again my question was irrelevant. "Well, it didn't traumatize you," my mother concluded, cutting dead any debate.

Paradoxically, I have Monsieur Plachet's rampant obscurantism to thank for an enduring passion for the mechanics of evolution and Darwinism, as well as an uncontrollable—and, I believe, childlike—rage whenever I hear the moronic ramblings of creationists. I also have him to thank for my lasting fascination with the Bible, with Genesis, Deuteronomy, and particularly Ecclesiastes, that poem of eternal wisdom that claims to have been written by a son of David, a searing text that I've read and reread, and that almost always brings tears to my eyes.

"All the rivers run into the sea, yet the sea is not full."

FOURTEEN

THE GREAT ESCAPE

You will be a great hero, a general,
Gabriele D'Annunzio, Ambassador of France!
This rabble doesn't know
who you are!

ROMAIN GARY, *PROMISE AT DAWN*

I was an average student at high school, happy simply not to fail. I was and still am naturally lazy, but my brain had all the qualities of a sponge. Given my facility with certain subjects, some people might have wrongly concluded that I took an interest in them. I wasn't bad at languages. I'd been familiar with English since my childhood in Surrey; I started German in sixth grade, and Russian in eighth grade. Whoever won the next war, I'd be ready to collaborate. I was keen to mimic the accents from Oxford, Lübeck, and Moscow as closely as possible, and I believe that in this doggedness there was a not particularly subconscious wish to be someone else.

For a long time I was "good at math," to the point that I went on to study the subject at college. But mathematics is implacable: like a butterfly that can fly through windowpanes, fluttering toward the light, you travel through one pane of glass, then another, until one final pane stands up to you, and you know it always will. Other butterflies join you at this unassailable frontier, and they cross it with no trouble. You then realize that, no, you're not all that good. And research isn't for you. No theorem will bear your name. You will, at best, be a mediocre intermediary, a teacher whose enthusiasm will eventually ebb away. That's life, as they say.

I'm not boasting—and this formula is always followed by a boast—but there was one class in which I immediately shone: philosophy. Here I proved my facility for manipulating concepts, and most of all I instantly enjoyed the principle of pressing a question until it released its juice. "Should we lose our illusions?" this subject asked. Why "should we"? What does it mean by "lose"? How to define "illusion"? Why the plural? Are they really *our* illusions? I truly loved it.

My teacher was called Jean-Louis Groma. He was tall and so stooped he looked hunchbacked; a clubfoot made him limp, and his face was angular, lean, almost bony. He wore a Groucho-style mustache under a long nose. I felt an instant admiration for him, and there's no doubt he genuinely was admirable, because he thought me rather talented. I discovered the benefits of the Pygmalion effect, the self-fulfilling prophecy that improves our performance because an acknowledged authority believes in us.

Groma was my second father figure, to use a concept from analysis, and, yes, his name began and ended like the word "Grandpa." On Thursdays, his lesson was the last of the morning, and I often stayed on so he could help me clarify a jumble of ideas. His diagnosis, when I was in senior year, was that I risked "turning into an old virtuoso," a subtle dig that, at just sixteen, flattered me. Nevertheless, he asked to meet my parents and insisted that I pursue this field with a foundation course in literature.

But my mother thought math was the only route to salvation. Hostage to her pride, I would triumph where her father had only dreamed of setting foot and where her first husband had failed: I would avenge them both and succeed at the École Polytechnique. But to get a place there, you have to want it, and really want it. I didn't want it very much. I was still a child, the monster that, as Sartre says, adults make with their regrets.

And until then this child had been naïve, happy, and, I think, unusually submissive to his mother. It wasn't until relatively late that I started questioning, arguing, confronting her. But I very soon realized I couldn't fight her, she couldn't tolerate any contradiction. The tiniest disagreement cast doubt on our relationship and—or this is how I experienced it—her love for me. Terrorized by this threat, I didn't allow myself to score even the smallest victory, and my brain invented the most bizarre way to stop itself from functioning.

Stupidity is a symptom, Françoise Dolto said. With me this symptom took the form of a lingering image of a tropical twilight: it's nightfall on a Pacific island, perhaps in the Galapagos atoll. In a moonlit chiaroscuro, a giant turtle has emerged from the ocean and is lumbering over a wide beach to dig a deep hole by the light of the moon. In it she lays her translucent mucousy eggs. Her pupils are moist and yellow; she weeps with the torment of turtle tears. Then her webbed hind limbs clumsily cover the eggs with sand.

It's a primitive, reptilian, universal scene. The image of the mater dolorosa, of the pain of childbirth—an image that has marked me forever. I must have watched this scene on my grandparents' black-and-white television in the sixties; it must have been late, or late for a child.

When I quarreled with my mother, the image of the marine reptile came to me. It confused all my lines of reasoning, erased all the arguments I had come up with. The turtle protected me, it stopped me triumphing over my mother, whom I would then have risked losing.

Then came one morning in February 1974. I had started my first year of advanced mathematics in a "good high school." I had embarked, as she so badly wanted me to, on the entry process for the prestigious "Grandes Écoles," to become an "engineer."

But on this particular day, although there's nothing to warn me of my imminent implosion, I can't take any more: I don't get off at the Métro station near my school, but a little farther along, at Odéon, and I walk toward the Jardin de Luxembourg. I unashamedly attributed this episode of my life to Thomas, the protagonist in an earlier novel. Why describe it any other way. Let's just switch to first-person narrative.

I walk beside the elongated pond, passing statues of the queens of France, and sit on a metal chair. I have prepared for this getaway: I have several books in my bag. It isn't at all cold.

In the evening I go home to my parents, starving: I had a baguette sandwich and a piece of fruit for lunch.

Over the ensuing week the park becomes my headquarters. I meet up with fellow bohemians: Manon, who is the same age as me and is skipping eleventh grade. The smell of patchouli will always remind me of her. Kader, a tall black guy of maybe thirty, a guitarist who plays in the Métro, and I sometimes go with him: when I do the begging for him, the combination of a white teenager and a black adult more than doubles the takings. If it rains, I shelter under one of the kiosks; if it's too cold, I move into the Malebranche, a smoky café where I meet friends from my foundation course at Louis-le-Grand. I talk politics and literature, and argue about Proust, Althusser, Trotsky, and Barthes, my vehemence in proportion to my ignorance of the texts. When I come to read them properly, later, I blush to remember the idiocies I uttered and marvel at the impunity of my imposture.

March comes, then April. I have informed my teachers that I've abandoned my studies. To my parents, of course, I lie. I discover how easy it is, exciting even, how gifted I am at lying. I reek of tobacco? I rant about how stressed smokers get before their practice exams. I'm short of money for lunch? From now on the cafeteria likes you to pay with cash; I say I suspect the bursar of corruption. I come home too early by mistake? An oxidation-reduction experiment went wrong and the chemistry teacher—"You're not going to believe this"—burned himself. I never talked about my studies so much until the day I quit them.

One May evening, almost before I've set foot in the house, I start elaborating that day's fiction. My father watches me, in silence. All at once my mother explodes. They know. The school called: I failed to return a book to the library, even though I defected three months ago. Angry words, flaring tempers, big arguments. I will never be admitted to one of the elite universities. My ungratefulness was utter and complete, in direct correlation with the sacrifices they'd been prepared to make. The return on their investment, so to speak, was pitiful. The atmosphere turned to lead.

Luckily, we had dinner with my grandmother every evening and my parents put on a brave face. But once we were home, back up the two floors, my mother restricted our exchanges to monosyllables and Guy, who wanted to demonstrate his total support for her, stopped talking to me altogether, crushing me with conspicuous contempt. I slunk off to my room and read. This went on a long time.

It was unbearable and yet when I left home a few months later, the day after my eighteenth birthday, they seemed completely bereft. I'd been planning it, I had a place to stay, at a friend's house, I'd packed my bag and saved up money. My mother flew into a towering rage. She threw my clothes and books into the street, tore up all the photographs she had of me, and cut me out of others where I featured, to make me disappear.

This meant war. But I hadn't wanted a breakdown in the relationship. I was helpless, unhappy, terrified by my own decision. I called my grandmother for news every day, or nearly. But I left neither a number where I could be contacted nor any indication of where I was living.

Still, on that April day in 1975, I did feel I'd stopped being my mother's property, and that I'd escaped her all-powerful hold. I didn't yet know that it was structural and I would escape its constraints so quickly.

I'll always remember one apocalyptic scene which for years made me blush right to my hairline: I was attending a lecture on analytical theory in amphitheater 24, at Jussieu, when I heard someone at the top of the section scream, "You bastard!" Everyone turned around. It was my mother. Paralyzed with horror, I watched her launch herself down the stairs like a banshee, in front of two hundred stunned students, momentarily distracted from the planes of Dirichlet series of absolute convergence. I stood up and tried to get away from her, but she hurled insults at me relentlessly, using filthy, almost incestuous words, the sort an abandoned mistress would keep specially for her young lover, so that some of my fellow students thought this had to do with a breakup.

I managed to drag her outside the amphitheater, but not to calm her down. It felt, as it always did with her, like fighting the Gorgon. Her shrieks reverberated around the vaulted ceiling, until her voice was reduced to a hiss, filled with loathing. When she ran out of arguments she moved on to threats. I should never try to come home again, I would never "extract a single cent from her," and I was "disinherited" anyway. I backed away, one step at a time; her fury was a black vortex and I didn't want to be swallowed up in it. Then, still beside herself, she marched away, leaving me shaking outside the amphitheater, which was starting to empty.

From that day on, I was careful to take the same courses but given in different amphitheaters, at different times of day and by different lecturers.

FIFTEEN

PIETTE'S DEATH

And there beyond grief
an open window,
a window streaming with light.
PAUL ÉLUARD, "ET UN SOURIRE," *LE PHŒNIX*

I don't have to justify myself for talking about Piette.
So, I wasn't yet twenty when I met Piette. It was
at a party I didn't want to go to, one of those slightly
pointless dinners given by students with slightly too much
time on their hands. There'd be too much drinking and
too much smoking, and it would often end with poker.
But at the far end of the table there was this very young
woman, Piette, this slim, almost skinny girl with delicate
features. I never discovered who invited her. She didn't
seem to know many people; she didn't know the names of
most people there.

Her eyes were green, the irises ringed with gray; she
had olive skin; her left temple was marked with a short,
fine scar, a tiny crescent moon like a trail of varnish. She
wore her black hair very short. I don't know if she was my

type at the time but she defined what my type would be in the years to come. "Go over to this woman," André Breton said, "and ask her whether the light in her eyes is for sale." I didn't have the guts.

With quick little movements, like someone steering a gaggle of geese with a stick, Piette directed the guests around that table. Every now and then she would throw out an idea—sometimes they were cutely absurd: "If I tell you not to think about elephants, what do you think about?"—and then leave everyone else to argue. She was quick to interrupt them the moment they threatened to become boring. She laughed and made people laugh, she was joyous and tragic, she filled me with enthusiasm and trepidation all at once. She was treading on a tightrope.

Piette's eyes never came to rest on me. A redheaded guy with freckles—I remember him as a giant—was with her. A Dane with a strong accent. From time to time he kissed her, took her hand awkwardly, as if to reassure himself he had her. The dinner plowed on, there was vanilla ice cream for dessert. She suddenly whispered something in his ear; he looked dumbstruck but she frowned at him, spoke just one more word, and he stood up abruptly and left the room. The door slammed. There was a brief pause at the table, looks were exchanged, Piette clapped her hands, said, "There was something rotten in the kingdom of *et cætera*," and conversation started up again. I realized she'd just dismissed him. I insisted we all share the Dane's ice cream, and she smiled at me, at last.

Piette lived in a large two-bedroom apartment near the Jardin des Plantes, the pied-à-terre of a rich young Australian whose mistress she had been, and who had gone back to live in London a month earlier. This seemed very exotic to me. When we reached her floor, there was an envelope on the doormat. It had keys inside it. She shrugged: "Oh look, keys." I thought I would be her new Dane. That was not what happened.

With Piette I discovered manic depression, bipolar disorder. The highs, when nothing and no one could challenge her omnipotence, and the lows too, when I feared for her life. I accepted her sickness, it was part of her; I accepted the symptoms, and the small suitcase of benzodiazepine and lithium nitrate.

"I never hate myself for the things I say or do when I'm down," she warned me one day. "You wouldn't resent me for puking if I had a stomachache. It's the same. It's my brain that's sick, not my thoughts."

Piette didn't much like my friends. Too militant, too sure of the workings of a too-readable world. I quickly accepted her disinclinations and overnight started seeing them less, then hardly ever. I loved life with Piette, first of all because I loved Piette. With her there were many more than twenty-four hours in a day and a night, and we spent them at the film library or reading poetry out loud or making love. Piette filled all my days, I was under her spell.

She very soon introduced me to her parents, Daniel and Claire, to her older brother, André, and her sister, Alice, all united around her against her sickness. Once again I was amazed by this family warmth, the mutual understanding, the obviousness of it. This wasn't just an only child's fascination for the pleasures of siblinghood. The cheerful simplicity that permeated their house was alien to me, the pleasure in being together that I had discovered as a young boy when visiting school friends. I had sometimes asked them about their lives, and projected myself into their happiness, imagined my life among these strangers who were so smiley and so open. I sometimes suspected I was kidding myself when I thought the grass really was greener on the other side of the fence. But it often was.

We had coffee. I was in the kitchen, having taken back the plates and glasses, when her mother took my hands and squeezed them, very hard. She said, "Thank you, thank you." I thought she was thanking me for helping clear the table, but she added, "You're someone for her."

I could see in her eyes that she hoped I would save Piette; her naïve newfound hope allowed me to believe I could. I went back to sit down next to Piette, who was laughing that husky, incredibly sensual laugh I've never found in anyone else.

Piette's family adopted me that day.

We'd been together only four months when Piette found she was pregnant. It was unexpected although foreseeable, or foreseeable although unexpected. Either way, it was good. I was not yet twenty and I was surprised by how ready I was. As for Piette, she wasn't in any doubt. At our regular Saturday lunch she announced her pregnancy to her parents. Claire wept with emotion. We uncorked the champagne; Piette drank only a drop.

Piette was happy, it was a joyful lunch, she wanted to get out the photo albums, and together we watched her childhood unfold through Polaroids. The family on the beach under a parasol, Piette crying great fat tears—she'd been stung by a jellyfish; André and Piette looking so proud on their skis; all the children dressed up for a costume party—Piette was the cartoon character Fantomette. In one photograph was a pink cake with five candles and chocolate sprinkles spelling out the six letters "P, I, E, T, T, E" rather well.

It was at the age of four that Rebecca Cohen stopped using her first name to become Piette. Little Rebecca had been read a story with a heroine called Miette, which means crumb (it was a symbolic story about a bakery, with lots of long, thin baguettes and big, round loaves, but the details don't matter much). Little Rebecca turned to her mother, her mind made up, and said, "I want people to call me Piette now." Claire tried to explain that a name was chosen for life but, confronted with the child's obstinacy, decided not to insist, convinced the whim would be short-lived. But in the space of a few months, Piette had persuaded everyone around her, refusing to react if anyone continued to call her Rebecca. The name in chocolate letters on that cake acknowledged her triumph.

At the time I had an old reflex camera, a Russian Zenit about as heavy as an anvil. I wasn't very gifted or very keen on souvenir snapshots—I was an "artist," like every-one else—but, encouraged by that episode with the photo album, I took picture after picture, a whole crop of them, for me and for this child to come, whose sex we didn't want to know. I accumulated masses of them in a cardboard box, not entirely sure what to do with them: Piette sitting in a chair grimacing prettily at her now very full breasts and her stomach, which was growing more rounded; Piette wandering those long legs of hers around the kitchen, draped in one of my shirts; Piette in a sensible wool dress, on a bench in a square, reading *Charlie Hebdo*; Piette naked on the bed with a funny felt hat on her head. It was, how can I put this, very "Godard." Sometimes, when I thought a photo was both good and Piette sufficiently covered up, I made a print of it for Daniel and Claire.

In an absurd symmetry and with little enthusiasm, I decided to introduce Piette to my mother and stepfather. They were going to be grandparents, the meeting seemed inevitable. I'd been gone nearly two years; our conversations were icy because, it went without saying, I was a bastard.

They suggested lunch at the La Lorraine brasserie on the place des Ternes. An impersonal, overpriced place that I hated. We met them there and my mother immediately asked Piette to say her name again.

"Piette," she said, and added, "I chose it when I was four."

"And your real name?" my mother asked.

"It is my real name," Piette replied.

Irritated, my mother couldn't help shrugging her shoulders; it was an imperceptible gesture, but Piette never missed a thing. She instinctively didn't like my mother, and found my stepfather significantly insignificant. My mother instantly loathed her. Courses came and went, banal questions proved that no one was interested in anyone else, I couldn't wait to get to the coffee, and we left quickly without mentioning the child on the way. That could happen another time.

On the first day of spring, as they did every year, Piette's parents had a gathering for their nearest and dearest at La Noche, their holiday house in Séguret to the south of Vaison-la-Romaine, and it was only much later that I realized "Noche" was an anagram of "Cohen." Piette had planned our "engagement" there: she would officially announce that she was expecting a baby. But I invited almost no one, and certainly not my mother or stepfather. Piette spared me from justifying this to Claire and Daniel.

"It's just for our family, Mom," she said. "There'll only be about twelve of us."

"It's such a shame," Claire said regretfully all the same, "it would be the perfect occasion."

There never was another.

Piette was four months pregnant when she threw herself under a train. An hour earlier she'd come out of the hospital in a western suburb of Paris, having asked to go in three days before that because one of her lows was just too hard, and the doctors had then felt she'd recovered enough to be discharged. She'd left a message on the answering machine, which I received much later: "Come get me, quickly, I love you." I didn't go to get her.

The health care center gave me the news that she was dead; the police had already contacted Claire and Daniel. I went to be with them, by taxi, and realized on the way there that I had no money to pay the fare. I got out, apologizing, with the driver cursing at me. When I arrived we spoke only a couple of words, no more. And for two days I stayed with them, in their home. Going back to my place, to our place, on rue Lacépède, would have been impossible for me. I don't remember much about those days, the noises from the street in the silence of the apartment, a mushroom omelet eaten in the kitchen with André, two nights on the guest bed, a dozen Maigret novels read until sleep knocked me out, for a few hours.

The funeral took place two days later.

André, Piette's brother, gave me a kippa, her mother tore my shirt on a level with my heart; my eyes had been almost dry until this hugely symbolic gesture for which I was unprepared. Tears sprang from my eyes and I had to go off alone for many long minutes to master myself.

I knew nothing of Jewish customs: Piette respected none of them, she loved saucisson and couldn't care less about the Sabbath. I'd hastily rehearsed some rituals and got lost and confused. I was awkward, burdened by myself. Daniel had to keep guiding my moves and showing me where I needed to stand. I was ashamed of my ignorance, constantly afraid I would shatter the dignity of the occasion with a blunder. I was a sort of Rabbi Jacob—a pathetic youthful version of him, and without the dancing intermissions. I threw a shovelful of earth on the coffin, just after her brother, who showed me that I should plant the shovel back into the loose earth, not hand it on. I discovered years later that in my circumstances, given that we weren't married and I wasn't a Jew, this was a form of tolerance as much as a mark of affection.

I hadn't for a single moment thought of asking my mother and Guy to come to the funeral with me. Guy would have worn that appropriately inscrutable expression that effectively masks indifference just as readily as stupidity, and my mother's sadness would have been so affected, so obviously manufactured that I'd have been ashamed of her. All I needed was truthfulness.

I was also afraid that whatever I managed to say to her she'd have brought flowers.

At the end of the ceremony, Piette's mother hugged me close.

"It's over. Thank you for being here. I mean: not just now. Earlier, for her."

And then she added, "It's better like this, you know. It was bound to happen. Later. Soon enough."

And also, "Don't vanish from our lives straightaway, please."

She opened her purse and handed me a small parcel wrapped in tissue paper. I opened it. It was a child's Swiss penknife, bright red with a white cross.

"Here," Claire said, "take it. It was Piette's when she was six or seven, it was the only knife she agreed to use for cutting meat and eating. I always used to tell her you have to eat to live. But to you I'll just say you have to live. In a year's time, on the anniversary of Piette's death, you'll be here. And by then I want you to have a new girlfriend, do you hear me. You're twenty. You have to live."

I followed her advice, I lived.

But first I listened, until I could hardly breathe, to Piette's voice in her last message. Much later, I burned all the photos I'd kept of Piette, and I threw away the box too, out of superstition I fear. I kept only one, in which she's lying on her stomach in a bubble bath, with just one foot emerging from the bubbles, a tiny matte black-and-white print, seven centimeters by ten centimeters; it went everywhere with me for a long time, in my billfold. And one day I lost the billfold.

I also lost the Swiss knife in the end.

That's the fate of all relics. To be venerated or lost.

The day after the funeral I decided to tell my mother Piette had died. And I do mean my mother, because I expected little more from my stepfather than some platitude at best. I rang their doorbell unannounced. My mother opened the door and was surprised to see me, almost anxious. I went in. I sat down in an armchair. It was a Pompadour-style chair, wooden framed and bucket shaped, but revisited by cubism, covered in sky blue velvet with a terribly busy pattern and embellished with pompoms and fringing, as things were in the seventies. My mother sat down facing me, on a sofa in the same style.

"Piette's dead," I said simply.

"Piette?" my mother asked, frowning.

The tone of voice didn't communicate stupefaction but incomprehension. She really had forgotten who this Piette was. So I explained.

"Piette. My girlfriend. We had lunch together. She's dead. She committed suicide."

My mother nodded.

"Oh yes," she said.

It was coming back to her.

"She did have a funny name, though," she added.

Bewildered, I didn't know what to say. I looked at the room around me, the velvet armchairs, the black-and-white cowhide under the black lacquered piano, the glass fronted bookcases, the heavy full-length silk curtains.

My stepfather, who was still standing, said nothing; he seemed to be staring at the dust on the piano. Suddenly he came over to me and whispered in my ear.

"Don't forget to wish your mother a happy birthday," he said. "It was three days ago and of course you forgot."

I now had an infallible way of remembering the day Piette died.

I stayed silent, stood up, asked to have a glass of water, and then headed for the door. To be absolutely honest, the memories I have of those brief minutes when I left are very unclear.

"Are you off already?" my stepfather must have said, angry that I was only there for that and had forgotten this wretched birthday. He must also have asked if I'd like to stay for lunch.

On the landing, I called the elevator, out of habit. My parents stood on the threshold. I didn't wait for the elevator and walked down the stairs, so that I could feel every step of those eight floors. My head was spinning.

I was annoyed with myself for going to see them. I felt no anger, except with myself. My mother's words had made it clear. I'd gone there only to be pitied. I was hoping for sympathy, condolences.

I realized I was indulging myself. I wanted to put on the cold black suit of the young widower, I was experiencing the "shrewd delight" derived from "the very causes of one's suffering," as described by Pessoa. I was ashamed of myself, I felt dirty, despicable. A real bastard, for once.

The very wise Jaime Montestrela wrote: "To the Hatu people, who live on the high plateau of Guadjapaja (in Mexico), in times of brutal bereavement, the words 'I share your pain' are never a metaphor. Everyone takes his or her share, and sometimes there is soon none left even for the individual who is meant to be suffering."

I no longer wanted to share my pain, with anyone.

I walked out of the building and sat at a table in the first café I came to. I ordered a macchiato. That's what Piette always drank.

It was years, decades rather, before I could mention Piette, and talk about her death. I managed it only when I knew I was no longer fishing for compassion, and the time of sadness was over.

And only then did I regret losing the Swiss knife.

· SIXTEEN ·

WAR AND PEACE

How come I'm a success
When my pedigree's such a mess?
JACQUES JOUET, *MEK-OUYES CHEZ LES TESTUT*

O f course I tried to make peace with my mother. Some wars just needed too much energy. Any sort of armistice was impossible, she had to see the rebel capitulate.

Purse-string blackmail is the nuclear weapon of parent-child conflicts. But I'd premeditated my getaway and organized myself to survive: years earlier, after my grandfather died, family Christmases had become the setting for a peculiar exchange of white envelopes. The three children—my two cousins and I—received very few presents but some money, accompanied by the ritual words: "You can buy something you really want." Logically, each child should have received the same amount, but my mother had a completely different way of reasoning and pointed out to Raphaëlle that she had only me while she, Raphaëlle, had two children. Consequently, my aunt, keen to avoid any arguments, gave me twice as much as each of my cousins received from my mother. Christmas had become a sort of family politics version of a zero-sum game. I didn't benefit much from this competitive advantage because the money was immediately put into a savings account. And one day it was all invested in a lock-up garage, which gave me a good "yield" because it was rented out.

The day I turned eighteen, I opened a new bank account and put all my savings into it. I hadn't forgotten that lock-up: I claimed the deeds for it and gave notice to the tenant. I wasn't very proud of this heist with its rather derisory spoils, but it saved my life for several months.

Sadly, even though I moved from one friend's house to another, gave math lessons, and briefly exercised a number of exotic and mostly nocturnal professions (a morgue attendant in Cochin, a copperplate image setter for *Libération* in the glory days of the rue de Lorraine, night watch person in a psychiatric clinic, hotel receptionist...) my stash was gradually exhausted.

Mathematics meant work; I couldn't see myself as much other than a teacher, and the day came when I had to hand myself over to the enemy in order to negotiate how my studies would be financed. My mother agreed to this but she chose humiliation: on every Sunday visit she gave me a small sum of money, barely enough to last the week, forcing me to come back and beg. I was no longer her son;

she was turning me into a sort of thankless venal gigolo, a torturer, with her as the victim.

This blackmail was not a good move: by demeaning me she demeaned herself; by making me ashamed of myself, she left me no choice but to distance myself.

Our relationship was still horribly violent.

One Sunday, after a fight about I don't even remember what, she drove me out of the house. I waited on the landing and she stood in the doorway with Guy behind her as logistical and moral support. I could see her anger rising, out of control. The elevator arrived and she lunged at me as the door was closing on me, but, unable to reach me with her hand, she lashed out with a foot and kicked me. I was so surprised I stood in stunned silence for a few seconds before the elevator set off. Alone in that cabin, I started by laughing. Then I was gripped by an icy feeling inside, swiftly followed by boundless rage. I pounded the metal walls with my fist; they were dented for many years to come.

For days she left insulting messages on my answering machine. Sometimes it was just a "Bastard!" or a "Shiiiiit!" screamed at the top of her lungs. I pictured Guy, somewhere close by, embarrassed in spite of everything, and, confronted with this immoderation, facing the prospect of trying to calm her.

I was only twenty-two, I couldn't take any more. I wrote her a letter intended to be conciliatory:

Mom,

I don't know why we always end up fighting, but I so wish it could stop happening.

First of all, because your criticism makes me sick with guilt. Also and most important because, contrary to what you think, I'm always sad I upset you. Unfortunately, since your insults always go hand in hand with threats, I don't think I can ever respond to them, because I wouldn't want you to think they've succeeded.

Mom, I love you. I don't know how to tell you, you'll also say I don't know how to show it, but each of your accesses and excesses of anger breaks me up, for a long time. I couldn't ever list all the things you criticize about me. I don't even know what I should do now to stop being the bastard you hate so much. You think this doesn't hurt me and I'm just indifferent. It's just that I suffer in my own way. I need you far more than you need me. You existed before me, you haven't always been my mother. I exist thanks to you and I've always been your son. Women are inevitably stronger than men, mothers stronger than sons. I may hurt you, but don't ever doubt that you can hurt me too.

You think I reject you. I don't reject you. I resist you, as all children do, and if I ever have a son or a daughter, he or she will resist me, when the time comes for confrontation. I'm not writing to criticize you in any way, or to list our differences, disagreements, and misunderstandings, but just to make peace, or to try to start to make peace.

I'm confronted with this wall of your anger, of your loathing even, and it hurts me. I don't know how to break it down.

I always feel that whatever I say will be thrown back in my face. So, try not to read this letter the wrong way or to twist what it's trying to say.

And give Dad a kiss from me. Make sure he knows I care.

A few days later I received a letter and recognized my mother's handwriting. The envelope said "Monsieur Hervé Le Tellier," which surprised me. Inside were about a hundred confetti-like shreds of paper. It was my letter, torn into tiny pieces.

I was devastated. I realized that my declaration had had no value for her. When I was barely eight years old she had made up her mind I was an ungrateful child and she'd decreed that I didn't love her. Nothing could have been further from the truth. Her voice had been full of cold anger and made me cry. She'd said it to me over and over, and in the end she was right.

By sending that letter, I'd been hoping for a gentle reply that would have given me the strength to rediscover the little-boy love that was now lost forever. But wanting to love is a far cry from loving. Perhaps when I made that final declaration I was actually hoping for only one thing: for her fury to abate, to have a little respite. So, yes, my very craven "Mom, I love you" probably did deserve that insult couched in confetti.

I never wrote to my mother again.

I didn't break off all contact with her, settling instead for seeing her less frequently. I didn't cover myself with glory by being so weak. I agreed to feel guilty and to behave as such, all the while suspecting that I was guilty of nothing.

Years went by, and our differences were constantly endorsed. I drew away from her, the way you might hold a stick of dynamite at arm's length; and she didn't make a single move toward me. My relationship with Guy, who followed her in every way, maintained its arctic tepidity. Eventually, answering machines evolved, but each new incarnation was treated to its own crop of "Bastard!" and "Shit!"

And I started to write.

My mother forced herself to appear proud, and my stepfather did too, displaying less contempt for me than I disguised for him. After all, his name appeared on the cover of each successive book.

And yet, in thirty years, neither he nor she read a single one, they never came to a reading, nor did they come to the theater to see any of my plays. I wasn't hurt: they didn't read anything and never went out, and my work—however admirable it may have been—wouldn't have succeeded in changing that.

Had they liked my work I would have been at best puzzled, at worst sad.

Writing was not the destiny my mother had in mind for me, and her pride suffered because she kept having to lower her ambitions for my career. Still, she never resigned herself to this: a doctorate achieved later in life found favor in her eyes; the fact that it was in linguistics was secondary. In fact, she never stopped asking what it was "in," and I tend to think this was due to genuine lack of interest rather than an early effect of her illness. In the end, I'd tell her whatever I felt like: molecular biology, health-related macroeconomics, particle physics (which raised a black look from Guy). When all was said and done, I was a doctor and only the title mattered. To this day, every time I visit her in the nursing home, she whispers, "Make sure the nurses know you're a doctor, it impresses them."

·
· ·

Honor your father and mother, that your days may be prolonged in the land which the Lord your God gives you," says Exodus, chapter 20, verse 12, and reiterates Deuteronomy in chapter 5, verse 16.

All translations of it are imprecise. For "honor," thesauruses suggest "celebrate," "glorify," "respect," and "adore." But a text doesn't release its moral as a lemon does its juice; this isn't about love or respect. The Hebrew word *kavod* (דובכ) has the same root as the adjective *kaved* (דבכ, "heavy"), and it means the more prosaic "bear the weight," "support," or "bear." So "support your father and mother" then. An indisputable commandment from Yahweh, a *mitzvah* straight out of a world without retirement homes or social security. Or it could be "Bear your father and mother."

I now bear my mother.

Matthew (15:4) says whoever curses his father and mother will be punished by death. But Matthew always exaggerates, he's one of those exalted types, and anyway, my mother has cursed me too much for me to have the strength to pass the buck back.

The last few years have seen her descend into madness. With Guy by her side it was possible to conceal the progress of Alzheimer's. Sure, there were signs: her inability to use a computer or a new telephone, which she disguised as a determined lack of interest or as frustration with anything new.

But in the week after her husband's death, I grasped the reality of this dementia and how much it would eat into my time. I now had the status of "caregiver," and this isn't the place to discuss how little provision is made to help the relatives of the sick. Neither do I want to describe her slow deterioration, the daily dramas, from losing her purse (which my son's mother had "stolen" from her) to the disappearance of the TV remote (which had been "hidden").

This intellectual decline increased her anxiety and paranoia: she took to calling me over a hundred times a day, leaving a message every time. Often to insult me, but also often to insult me because she'd forgotten she'd insulted me. The voice-mail service from my provider soon gave up the ghost, saturated with hours of messages. I stopped picking up, stopped listening, made do with calling her regularly to appease her, only starting to worry if half a day went by without her leaving a message.

One time she asked me if her father was dead, and when he'd died. I told her it was nearly fifty years ago.

"Why do you tell me filthy lies like that?" she retorted nastily. "I saw Daddy yesterday."

The time came when she took to stopping people in the street to ask them to call me or send a text. Our exchanges were bizarre and the spelling fluctuated depending on the victim:

"Your mothers trying to get hold of you. Call her."

"Thank you for your message. I'll call her. But I've already spoken to her twice this morning…"

"Oh, she said she been trying to reach you since yesterday evening."

"Yep. I also spoke to her eight or ten times yesterday."

"Rite, I'm so sorry. I just met her in the street."

Her body didn't let her down: like a headless chicken, she could walk through the streets for hours, always on the same circuit with clearly delineated stages.

In a single day she could go into the bank a half dozen times to withdraw cash, and to the delicatessen ten times, insisting they call me because she had "no money left to eat." She became a pest to the people in her apartment building, whose doorbells she would ring at all hours, and to the janitor, whom she woke in the night and who couldn't take any more. I also had regular conversations with the police.

Therapeutic internment was soon the only solution. Then, after a suspension of medication, a specialized establishment.

My mother wanted to get out, to go home, even though she'd forgotten where she lived and couldn't even locate her own room. It was now impossible to leave her alone for a moment, but she still had her arguments:

"People are so dumb, if you only knew, they don't know a verb from a complement."

To make the transition less distressing, I'd brought a dresser, a reclaimed piece from her old apartment. A few ivory ornaments too, in a locked display cabinet. Like having a toad in a vivarium, I reconstituted her habitat. I also gathered up some photos: her parents, my son, me, and even Guy, who had the progress of her illness to thank for a sort of return to favor.

One Sunday when I visited her the pictures had disappeared.

"She tore them all up," the nurse told me regretfully. "Into tiny little pieces. We couldn't save them."

I didn't understand. She so loved her parents.

At first I thought it pained her too much seeing them there when they were no longer alive.

Then I realized she resented them: not only had the living deserted her, but even the dead had abandoned her.

SEVENTEEN

THE OLD COUPLE

Love. To be totally banned.
It never comes without emotion.
Emotions are detrimental to consistency.
ALEXANDRE VIALATTE, *CHRONIQUES DE LA MONTAGNE*

I t was the last summer when my mother could still be left alone, when the illness didn't necessitate constant surveillance.

She and I were having lunch yet again at the Wepler. This brasserie on the place de Clichy is one of those establishments where the waiters have a knack for being familiar yet respectful, thoughtful yet discreet. The premises lend themselves to it. Henry Miller and Boris Vian had tables there, and Jacques Roubaud sometimes breakfasted there. When it rains in winter the square can look like a painting by Caillebotte. The horse-drawn carriages have gone.

We were sitting inside, on a raised area by the window. My mother had asked to have a table in this area, for the golden light that bathed it, but she was now complaining about being there because the sun was bothering her. We swapped places, but the heat was troubling her too and she had put her sunglasses back on so the maître d' would notice her considerable discomfort. I was embarrassed, but I was used to that. Apparently, you can be said to have shaken off all nationalistic feeling when you're no longer ashamed of your fellow countrymen abroad. In the same way, embarrassment was my last link to my mother.

She was singing to herself, as she often did, without really realizing she was. I recognized the little three-step dance tune whose lyrics so perfectly encapsulated her philosophy: "I piss off half the world (*repeat*) and I shit on the other half." Sartre quoted it in *Troubled Sleep*: this was my mother's way of being existentialist.

She had ordered the set menu, the "butcher's choice cut." Whatever the menu, my mother always had steak frites. This meant some restaurants were excluded: any attempt to make her try Indian, Chinese, or Lebanese cuisine, in short to taste food that was even a tad exotic, was a searing disaster (if I can venture that pun). A steak, then; rump, sirloin, filet, rib, porterhouse, the terminology didn't matter much, it just had to be red meat. She always asked specifically for it to be medium rare, but in my experience it was never cooked enough and it was almost invariably sent back to the kitchen. And when it reappeared it was "shoe leather" and she ate only the inside.

My mother sorely strained waiters' professionalism.

She could have been used as a test customer in catering schools. Put simply, my mother was difficult.

We were seated next to an old couple, or let's say a couple of old people. Their coupledom could in fact have been young but they were old people. I'm well aware that the word "old" has become politically incorrect, physiologically inaccurate, and relatively unpindownable. How old are the old people in Alphonse Daudet's *Les Vieux*? Let's establish that my old people were seventy-five, which means that in fifteen years' time they'll seem a lot less old.

The place Clichy is at the intersection of four Paris arrondissements with clear-cut, contrasting personalities. Our table neighbors were more middle-class types from the Eighth Arrondissement than working-class from the Thirteenth. He in a light gray suit, with white hair, she in a violet-colored suit, her hair set in a chestnut brown perm. One would guess he was wearing Dior's Eau Sauvage and she Nina Ricci's L'Air du Temps.

They gazed at each other tenderly, as they say in novels. With an empathy that was still fresh, although it didn't seem new, something they'd managed to preserve despite the years. The man leaned toward the woman and very lightly brushed her cheek with the back of his hand. She smiled, closed her eyes, and tilted her head prettily against his caress.

It was an exquisitely youthful moment, a snapshot of shared sensitivity that said we're ageless, even if realities of the body sometimes reclaim possession of us.

The man's gesture didn't go unnoticed by my mother.

She hardly looked up from her plate and hissed quietly, for my ears only, "Stupid old asshole, so stupid."

I knew instantly that she meant just him, and not them. Not for a moment, I realize now, did I think she might have sibilated another "s" at the end of the word.

Completely proving my first impression, she almost immediately added, "Well…good for her."

I didn't reply. My mother had always said what she meant, and meant what she said. Arguing was pointless. Guy had also always been "a stupid asshole." In fact, not a day had gone by when she hadn't struck him that particular blow.

She often added with a contemptuous sigh, "Rather the devil you know…" Incapable of being on her own, my mother had opted to be with just anybody.

The two old lovers next to us were smiling as they drank their coffee. Together they triumphed over time; they almost made you want to grow old.

I wondered whether, had he been a young man, my mother would simply have said "Stupid asshole." Whether it was his age that made him a stupid asshole, or quite simply his love. I'm inclined to go for the second option. A man who loves is a stupid asshole. A woman who loves is a stupid bitch. What a fuck-up love is. My mother had her own way of paraphrasing Prévert.

And my sentimental education still goes on.

· EIGHTEEN ·

ALL HAPPY
FAMILIES

*All happy families are
alike. Every unhappy family
is unhappy in its own way.*
TOLSTOY, *ANNA KARENINA*

I don't know whether Tolstoy is right.

I've never wanted to have a different family, and it was only long after I escaped it that I considered whether mine was unhappy. I was obscurely aware that something wasn't right, and at a very early stage I wanted to leave. And, also at a very early stage, I did leave. There was too little father in my stepfather, no father at all in my father, and too much fakery and unhealthy love in my mother.

When I made my escape, I didn't really feel any heartbreak. I never had a strong desire to fit myself into some line of descent. If I'd been a Jew, an Arab, or black, what do I know, the temptations of this sense of belonging could well have been stronger. For lack of reflection on the subject,

I might have been driven to asserting how "proud" I was to be just that, a Jew, an Arab, or black—a blood-related patriotism that, in terms of stupidity, is on a par with the land-related sort. But no: as a white Catholic boy born in Paris, I had no claims to be exotic, and I was spared any feeling of pedigree thanks to the weakness of my ancestry and its failure to have anything worth passing on. And anyway, had I been a Jew I would have had a Jewish mother.

I don't see myself as belonging anywhere. I've decided to be nothing—which, I have to confess, requires little effort—and to enjoy that fact, because it strikes me that this is protection from any fantasy of identity. I realize that you could argue the exact opposite, that we can only be fully open to other people if we're grounded on a solid base. But belonging is a slippery slope, and the mental stability of people who draw up family trees—people who want to depend on something, to look back as much as forward—has always struck me as shaky. The pretentious ramifications of these family constructs remind me of frantic imprints left in the snow by animals trying to escape predators. I feel much happier knowing that, eight hundred million years ago, the ancestor I have in common with the starfish was an animalcule with no anus.

Even so, when my partner read this, she said, "Hey, don't let people think you don't owe anything to anyone, because that's not possible. Unless I'm wrong, it does happen sometimes, or if you really think you have nothing to thank your family for, then at least explore that, say something about it. Either way...I'm pretty sure that, as usual, you'll do whatever pleases you."

Of course she's right—which happens a lot with her. I'm cobbled together, she knows that, held together with bits of string, and I owe so much to so many people that I couldn't name them all. So how could I have taken nothing from my mother, my very absent father, and even Guy? But that's another story and, yes, I do exactly what pleases me.

I don't recognize myself in books about mothers. François Mauriac wants revenge, Albert Cohen to be forgiven, Romain Gary to be consoled. There's no greater taboo than lovelessness and estrangement. Maybe nothingness isn't a subject.

That's not entirely true. I'm pretending, making a show of indifference. We never escape what we have lacked. I had far too much mother as it was to want another one, but I did dream of other fathers.

I dreamed of a father on the run. He would drop in to see me secretly to escape his killers or the police; he would stay by my bedside and describe his adventures to me in a hushed voice before leaving through the window.

I dreamed of a father who worked the land. A taciturn man who came in late and leaned over to wish me goodnight when I was already asleep, he smelled of cowsheds, and it was this smell hanging in the darkness that told me he'd been there.

I dreamed of an admirable father, immersed in work that I didn't understand at all. He would sit at his desk writing by lamplight, then suddenly look up at me, and smile.

I dreamed of pure, straightforward love, given unreservedly, unconditionally. When I became a father myself, I immediately knew there was no other kind.

Love. In *Journey to the End of the Night*, Céline wrote: "I'd definitely felt, plenty of times, that there was love in reserve. There's loads of it. You can't say there isn't. It's just a shame people are still so nasty when there's so much love in reserve. It doesn't get out, that's all. It's caught up inside, it stays inside, it's no good to them. It's killing them inside, this love is."

As a teenager, I copied out those sentences in my notebook of quotes, a yellow spiral-bound pad—and the fact that Céline got it so right when he himself was so contemptible remains a mystery to me. I agreed. I still do. And if I so wanted communism to succeed, it was not only because it promised equality and justice, but also because it would have allowed the love in all of us to be fully expressed. Perhaps deep down it's two sides of the same coin.

.
. .

I often think about the last scene in Truffaut's film *Small Change*. It's Truffaut himself speaking through the character of the primary school teacher Richet, played by Jean-François Stévenin. A child called Julien has been physically abused, beaten by his family, and he's going to be "put in care." The children are about to break up for the summer vacation, some will be leaving the school and moving on to junior high, and Mr. Richet talks to them: "In a strange sort of balance, those who've had a difficult childhood are often better equipped to tackle adult life than those who've been protected or very loved. It's a sort of law of compensation. Later in life you'll have children, and I hope you'll love them and they'll love you. In fact, they'll love you if you love them. Otherwise, they'll transfer their love, their affection or tenderness onto other people or other things. Because life is made so that we can't get by without loving and being loved."

I wasn't a deprived, beaten, or abused child like little Julien. I'm not complaining. I know what I owe to my strange family, I know what I owe to its deficiencies and what to its excesses.

If we spend our lives filling the voids opened in our childhood, then I know why I so love laughter, which only ever made its way into our house by breaking and entering; why I never stop finding elective families for myself; and why my friends mean so much to me.

There's also how fragile I am, my hypersensitivity. Louis Jouvet used to tell his students, "Be moving, not moved." But I can't do it. Too often when I give a reading, my voice goes flat, my throat constricts, my nose gets clogged, my eyes mist over, and I struggle to contain my tears.

It's an embarrassing predicament. I've tried to identify what upsets me, to pick out the fault lines through which this excess emotion spills out. I'm the man who can bury a friend without overflowing with tears, but I'm incapable of reading to the end of certain passages out loud: Ecclesiastes, or Aragon's poem "The Rose and the Reseda" ("The one who believed in heaven, the one who didn't…"), or a list of names of people whose desperate fates I know. Something inside me snaps and I have to break off. But I've decided that this crack in my makeup may also be my strength, and that it's through these fissures that life gets inside me.

I know that—because I couldn't live in my parents' world nor in the world as it was, because I couldn't breathe there—I wanted to change it, and later came the urge to invent another world, my world, my subjective creation, into which I could take other people. Writing is, so to speak, my privilege, allowing me to benefit from the world several times over, and endlessly savor my own dissatisfaction.

My father and stepfather are dead, my mother is mad. They won't read this book, and I felt I finally had the right to write it.

I don't know what it might mean to anyone other than me. But by putting words to my story, I've understood that sometimes a child's only choice is escape, and at the risk of being fragile, he will have this escape to thank for loving life all the more.

CREDITS

Epigraph on page 35 from *La Place de l'Étoile* by Patrick Modiano, translated by Frank Wynne in *The Occupation Trilogy* (NY: Bloomsbury, 2015). Epigraph on page 43 from Molière's *The Learned Women*, translated by Charles Heron Wall. Lyrics on page 45 from "C'est si bon," music by Henri Betti, lyrics by André Hornez, Colombia, 1948. Copyright © Peermusic Publishing, Beuscher Arpege. Epigraph on page 67 by Louis-Ferdinand Céline from *L'Église*, and excerpt on page 170, translated in *Céline: Journey to the End of the Night* by John Sturrock (NY: Cambridge University Press, 1990). Excerpt on pages 81–82 from *Les Misérables* by Victor Hugo, translated by Lee Fahnestock and Norman MacAfee. Copyright © Lee Fahnestock and Norman MacAfee, 1987. Published by Signet Classics, New York. Lyrics on page 86 from "Flower Duet" in the opera *Lakmé* by Léo Delibes, 1883. Epigraph on page 131 from *Promise at Dawn*, by Romain Gary, translated by John Markham Beach (NY: New Directions, 1987). Quotes on page 151 from "Letter to Mário de Sá-Carneiro, 14 March 1916" in *The Selected Prose of Fernando Pessoa*, translated by Richard Zenith (NY: Grove Atlantic, 2002).

HERVÉ LE TELLIER is a writer, journalist, mathematician, food critic, and teacher. He has been a member of the Oulipo group since 1992 and one of the "Papous" of the famous France Culture radio show. His books include *A Thousand Pearls (for a Thousand Pennies)*, *Enough About Love*, and *Eléctrico W*.

ADRIANA HUNTER studied French and Drama at the University of London. She has translated more than fifty books including Camille Laurens's *Who You Think I Am* and Hervé Le Tellier's *Eléctrico W*, winner of the French-American Foundation's 2013 Translation Prize in Fiction. She lives in Kent, England.

▞ OTHER PRESS

You might also enjoy these titles by Hervé Le Tellier:

ENOUGH ABOUT LOVE

Any man—or woman—who wants to hear nothing—or no more—about love should put this book down.

"What could be more romantic than falling in love in Paris? Unless you are already married, in which case it's a little more complicated…Le Tellier writes about middle-aged desire and its consequences with empathy and humor." —*Washington Post*

"At least as intriguing as how the French make their bread taste so good is how they manage all those extramarital love affairs they're said to have." —*New York Times*

ELÉCTRICO W

This brilliant and witty novel set in Lisbon explores love, relationships, and the strange balance between literature and life.

"[A]n engaging snapshot of these [characters'] briefly intersecting lives."
—*New York Times Book Review*

"[T]old with an earnestness that we see less and less of in novels in America. Le Tellier might remind readers of Roberto Bolaño; both feature a poetic melancholy and characters that understand the world through the prism of literature." —*Daily Beast*

Additionally recommended:

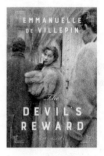

THE DEVIL'S REWARD
by Emmanuelle de Villepin

Three generations of women untangle a family history that spans both world wars and reveals unexpected insights about marriage and fidelity.

"Gracefully highlights the ways people of widely varying temperaments learn to coexist... features gratifyingly in-depth character studies and a strong sense of place." *—Booklist*

THE SONGS by Charles Elton

A painful choice made sixty years earlier by folk legend Iz Herzl leaves an indelible mark on the next generation.

"This is a truly wonderful novel — heartbreaking, funny, and such a painful dissection of family life it makes one wince." —Deborah Moggach, author of *The Best Exotic Marigold Hotel*

WHAT YOU DID NOT TELL: A FATHER'S PAST AND THE JOURNEY HOME
by Mark Mazower

A warm and intimate memoir by an acclaimed historian that explores the European struggles of the twentieth century through the lives, hopes, and dreams of a single family — his own.

"There are few historians who can write as grippingly as Mazower about secrets and the painstaking work of revealing them."
—Financial Times

OTHER PRESS

www.otherpress.com